TALL SHIPS TODAY
THEIR REMARKABLE STORY

Published by Adlard Coles Nautical
an imprint of Bloomsbury Publishing Plc
50 Bedford Square, London WC1B 3DP
www.adlardcoles.com

Bloomsbury is a trademark of Bloomsbury Publishing Plc

First published by Adlard Coles Nautical in 2014

ISBN 978-1-4729-0346-4
ePDF 978-1-4729-0348-8
ePub 978-1-4729-0347-1

A CIP catalogue record for this book is available from the British Library.

This book is produced using paper that is made from wood grown in managed, sustainable forests. It is natural, renewable and recyclable. The logging and manufacturing processes conform to the environmental regulations of the country of origin.

Typeset in Haarlemmer MT by James Watson
Printed and bound in China by C&C Offset Printing Co.

Note: while all reasonable care has been taken in the publication of this book, the publisher takes no responsibility for the use of the methods or products described in the book.

10 9 8 7 6 5 4 3 2

TALL SHIPS TODAY
THEIR REMARKABLE STORY

NIGEL ROWE
RON DADSWELL, COLIN MUDIE & MICHAEL RAUWORTH

CONTENTS

1 ORIGINS AND EVOLUTION
THE HISTORY AND DEVELOPMENT OF SAILING SHIPS COLIN MUDIE

2 THE TALL SHIPS
THE GLAMOUR AND DIVERSITY OF TALL SHIPS SAILING TODAY

INTRODUCTION MICHAEL RAUWORTH

THE SHIPS NIGEL ROWE

I very much welcome the publication of this splendid book. The benefits of training young people to manage 'tall ships' at sea have been argued for years. However, no-one has ever questioned the nature of the challenge of life at sea under sail to young people growing up in the comforts of modern life. Many young people are still severely disadvantaged in this 'high-tec' world, but the problems are created by human enterprise. Life at sea in a sailing ship is a contest with natural forces, which can only be won by knowledge, skill and determination.

Sail Training International has given many thousands of young people the chance to experience the satisfaction of learning how to use the natural elements to reach a destination across the ocean by the team management of sails in every kind of weather conditions. There is nothing quite like the satisfaction of arriving at the chosen destination after a hard passage, or at the end of a close-run race.

There are some spectacular photographs in this book, but they cannot convey the real thing. That has to be experienced 'live', but the effect such an experience has on the young crews of these ships is all too evident to those who have known them before and after their time at sea.

INTRODUCTION & ACKNOWLEDGEMENTS

Putting this book together has involved many people around the world telling the story of today's tall ships and sail training.

Although a key focus of the book is to give an insight into more than 100 of the world's most interesting tall ships sailing today, it is much more than a 'fleet review'. The publishers and I wanted to produce the definitive story of the tall ships: their origins and evolution, what it is like to sail on them, and the whole experience of racing on them – for the crews and the ports that host them. We also wanted to strike a balance between making the book an easy read for people who know little or nothing about tall ships as well as for the tall ship 'groupies' who have already had the wonderful experience of sailing on them.

Chapter One (*Origins and Evolution*) looks back over the long and fascinating history of the development of sail. It began a few thousand years ago with hollowed-out trees and reed hulls with animal skins or woven material hung on a pole to catch the wind. Over time, man's ingenuity, new materials and technologies enabled the construction of very sophisticated vessels, big and strong enough to carry cargoes, armaments and large crews across oceans.

Chapter Two (*The Tall Ships*) demonstrates the incredible diversity of the tall ship fleet currently at sea, with many vessels having interesting histories before they became sail training ships as well as some built specifically for the purpose. This diversity also extends to the extraordinary voyages many have undertaken and the huge number of young trainees who have had a life-changing experience sailing on them.

Chapter Three (*The Tall Ship Experience*) tells the story of a young man undertaking his first sail training voyage on a tall ship. It also explores the purposes and value of sail training, as well as the work that has been undertaken in recent years to improve at-sea safety regimes, the efficacy of on-board training and programmes to protect the marine environment.

Chapter Four (*Racing on Tall Ships*) takes the tall ship and sail training experience into the uniquely challenging environment of friendly competition and cultural exchange. The tall ships races and regattas organised by Sail Training International enable ships of different sizes and heritages to race on equal terms. They bring together young people from many different countries, cultures, backgrounds and abilities to share the experience and promote international friendship and understanding. They also provide a spectacle and festive atmosphere for the many hundreds of thousands of visitors to each host port when the fleet is in. It is these events more than any other activity that earned Sail Training International its nomination for the Nobel Peace Prize in 2007.

Everyone involved in producing the content of this book (text, photographs and other illustrations) has donated their time, talent and work at no cost to the project. As a result, all income for Sail Training International from sales of the book around the world will be used to help young people who are disadvantaged and/or disabled to benefit from the tall ship experience.

If this book inspires you, just consider the observation of His Royal Highness the Duke of Edinburgh in his comments on page 6: 'There are some spectacular photographs in this book, but they cannot convey the real thing. That has to be experienced 'live'.'

Most of the ships featured in Chapter Two would be delighted to welcome you on board!

Drawing on the knowledge and understanding of the three other contributing authors, all experts in their field (see pages 10 and 11), has ensured that this book is authoritative. **Ron Dadswell**, **Colin Mudie** and **Michael Rauworth** have a deep understanding of the various aspects of tall ships and sail training. Ron has also been a valuable help to me in putting the book together, well beyond the chapter he has written. I am also grateful to Colin for producing a good deal of original artwork to illustrate his chapter. Thanks also to **Paul Bishop**, head of Sail Training International's race directorate, for the artwork on pages 36 and 37 and for running his expert eye over the write-ups of the ships featured in Chapter Two. Valuable administrative support in the planning stages for the book was provided by **Esther Tibbs**.

Some of Sail Training International's member **national sail training organisations** played a pivotal role in securing the co-operation of ship operators featured in Chapter Two. Most of the photography in this chapter, and some of it in the rest of the book, has come from the operators of the ships featured. Some, particularly in Chapter Four, have also come from Sail Training International's archives. But I have also had open access to the work of five well-known and internationally respected tall ship photographers: **Herbert Boehm** (www.sail-and-travel.de), **John Cadd** (www.ships-shapes.com) **Max Mudie** (www.tallshipstock.com), the late **Thad Koza** (asta@tallshipsamerica.org) and **Valery Vasilevskiy** (www.photonord.ru). Max and Herbert were particularly helpful in also shooting some additional photographs exclusively for the book. My thanks also to **Alexander Ravn** who kindly volunteered to be the 'model' to illustrate the story of a trainee's experience in Chapter Three.

Together with the photographs submitted by the operators of the ships featured in Chapter Two, we had more than 3,000 photos to review and select from. The biggest single task in putting the book together has in many ways therefore been collating the photography and other illustrations, particularly for Chapter Two, and this task was undertaken primarily by **Julia Rowe**.

Collaboration with Bloomsbury Publishing's commissioning editor **Liz Multon** on developing both the concept of the book and its content has been both critical and a joy. So too has been working with designer **James Watson**, bearing in mind how important design is to a book like this, and **Jenny Clark** who co-ordinated the actual production of the book for Bloomsbury.

Everyone who had a part in putting this book together joins me in thanking particularly **HRH The Duke of Edinburgh** for his generous comments and endorsement on page 6. His Royal Highness has had a close association with experiential learning, sail training and tall ships from an early age. As a boy, he attended Gordonstoun School in Scotland when it was led by the world-renowned pioneer of experiential learning Kurt Hahn. In 1956 he was patron of the first ever Tall Ships Race from Torbay, England, to Lisbon, Portugal. In the late 1960s Kurt Hahn enlisted His Royal Highness's help in finding sponsorship for a new youth training ship, launched in 1971 as the *Captain Scott*. For many years His Royal Highness was patron of the UK's Sail Training Association and in 2006 he was patron and official starter of the Torbay to Lisbon 50th Anniversary Tall Ships Race organised by Sail Training International (see Chapter Four).

Nigel Rowe OBE
Patron, Sail Training International
June 2014

ABOUT THE AUTHORS

Nigel Rowe OBE is the editor and main author of the book. He wrote the background stories on the ships featured in Chapter Two (*The Tall Ships*) and Chapter Three (*The Tall Ship Experience*). He also edited the whole text for the book as well as being responsible for the initial selection of photographs and other illustrations for the designer to work with. A former trustee of the UK Sail Training Association (1998–2001), he was appointed deputy chairman of the International Sail Training Association (a subsidiary of the UK STA) in 1999, then chairman in 2000. He led the creation of Sail Training International as an independent organisation in 2002 and became its first chairman and president. When he retired from these positions in 2012 he was appointed patron. Nigel's prior career was in journalism, public affairs and corporate management. He is the author of two other books, one on the art and practice of business communications, the other on his participation in the 1994–1995 single-handed round-the-world yacht race. Nigel was awarded an OBE in the 2013 New Year's Honours for 'services to charity'.

Ron Dadswell OBE, the author of Chapter Four (*Racing on Tall Ships*), has 40 years' experience of sail training and tall ships, from trainee to chief officer. He was race director for The Tall Ships Races 1992–1995 and has served as chairman on a number of tall ships race committees. He was chairman of the UK's Association of Sail Training Organisations from 2001 to 2010 and is a founding trustee of Sail Training International. Ron's first career was as a navigating officer in the Merchant Navy, followed by 25 years in the British Army from which he retired as a colonel. Ron was awarded an OBE in the 2007 Queen's Birthday Honours for 'services to sail training'.

Colin Mudie RDI, CEng, FRINA, Hon FRIN, FRSA, the author of Chapter One (*Origins and Evolution*), is an internationally renowned naval architect and yacht designer. Several of the tall ships featured in Chapter Two were designed by him: STS *Lord Nelson*, TS *Royalist*, INS *Sudarshini*, INS *Tarangini*, KLD *Tunas Samudera* and STS *Young Endeavour*. He also designed the world's smallest square-rigged ships (the nine-metre *Bob Allen* and *Caroline Allen*) and the largest (the 200-metre vessel illustrated on pages 26 and 27). Yachts, motor boats and expedition vessels are among Colin's many other designs and he is the author of several books on the design and operation of sailing ships and other vessels.

Michael Rauworth wrote the introduction to Chapter Two (*The Tall Ships*). He has been a board member of Tall Ships America, the US national sail training organisation, since 1992 and its chairman since 2002. He has had a lifelong association with seagoing pursuits, including some 200,000 nautical miles as a professional deck officer or master on more than 20 commercial and military vessels (among them the sail training tall ships USCG *Eagle*, *Sea Cloud*, *Spirit of Massachusetts* and *Westward*). Mike is a practising lawyer specialising in maritime and admiralty matters. He is also a lecturer at the Massachusetts Maritime Academy in the USA.

ABOUT SAIL TRAINING INTERNATIONAL

Sail Training International is the international voice of sail training. It is a UK-based non-profit organisation whose members are the national sail training organisations of some 30 countries around the world. Its mission is the development and promotion of sail training for young people. It develops 'best practice' guidelines for on-board safety, training programme content and protection of the marine environment. It is the world's only organiser of international races and regattas for sail training tall ships. It also organises conferences and seminars, produces various publications and sponsors research. Underpinning much of Sail Training International's work is a focus on international understanding and friendship for which it was nominated for the Nobel Peace Prize in 2007.

Sail Training International was created in 2002 as an independent organisation by most of those involved at the time with the International Sail Training Association (ISTA). ISTA organised The Tall Ships Races in Europe and was a subsidiary of the UK's Sail Training Association. Sail Training International was established to fulfil the much broader mission outlined above. It acquired the assets of ISTA in 2002 and was granted charitable status in 2003.

Sail Training International

... the international voice of sail training
... changing young people's lives

Sail Training International
Charles House – Gosport Marina
Mumby Road
Gosport
Hampshire PO12 1AH
UK
W www.sailtraininginternational.org
E office@sailtraininginternational.org

Members of Sail Training International are the national sail training organisations of Australia, Belgium, Bermuda, Canada, Croatia, Czech Republic, Denmark, Estonia, Finland, France, Germany, Greece, Hungary, India, Ireland, Italy, Latvia, Lithuania, the Netherlands, New Zealand, Norway, Poland, Portugal, Russia, South Africa, Spain, Sweden, UK and USA.

FOREWORDS

The remarkable story of tall ships today is also the remarkable story of sail training and its uniquely valuable contribution to the lives of hundreds of thousands of young people around the world. In the middle of the last century most people believed the age of sail had come to an end. The Tall Ships Race organised in 1956 was designed to be a final farewell. In fact it heralded a renaissance for sailing ships, not only as a key element in the training programme for those seeking a career at sea but also for the personal development of civilian youth and a voyage of adventure for people of all ages. This book tells the story of tall ships and sail training in a way that has not been done before.

Douglas Prothero
Chairman
Sail Training International

Tall ships epitomise the glamour, majesty and romance of the sea and a bygone age. Yet there is a huge international fleet of tall ships still sailing today, some more than a century old, others built in just the last few years. Their origins and evolution give a fascinating perspective on the development of international maritime trade and conflict as well as developments in design, technology and navigation. Today the tall ships provide a unique opportunity for adventure at sea for people of all ages, backgrounds and abilities. Most also serve a vital and unique purpose in today's world beyond this. A voyage on a tall ship develops important 'life' and 'employability' skills, particularly in the young. They are also used by maritime academies (merchant and military) to help train young people for a career at sea. And they provide a dramatic spectacle in port that attracts wide public attention among people who have no other interest at all in the sea.

Spectacular photography of the tall ships at sea and in port, with key information on the vessels and their voyages, make this a unique reference work as well as a fascinating book to read or just look through.

Sir Robin Knox-Johnston CBE
International Goodwill Ambassador
Sail Training International

COLIN MUDIE

ORIGINS AND EVOLUTION

THE HISTORY AND DEVELOPMENT OF SAILING SHIPS

As steam took over from sail: *The square-rigged wool clipper* Argonaut *under full sail and running before the wind, with the P&O steamer* Mooltan *in her wake astern*. Artist Jack Spurling 1925. Sourced from Wikimedia Commons

The recorded history of mankind at sea extends back more than 4,000 or 5,000 years. Sailing ships and the exploration of the oceans have been arguably the greatest and most valuable of man's technical triumphs considering the available materials and the bravery involved in early seafaring. Some of the early vessels were conceived and built by pioneers of the same mental calibre as those who built the temples and cathedrals that have survived down the centuries and at which we still wonder. These technical advances were the product of exceptional brains and intelligence of the kind we now set to work on today's miracles of science and engineering. The main differences in our approaches over the centuries lie in the materials and technology at our disposal and the knowledge base of the time. The bravery of those who explored the unknown oceans in those early days of sail, often with little certainty of survival let alone return, is certainly on a par with those engaged in risky endeavours of more recent times, both on land and in space.

EARLY SEAFARING

The ships of antiquity had normally a rather short life – possibly some 20 years for a wooden ship before the rot and worm finished her, quite apart from a possible life of peril and danger on the great seas. Ships built from reeds had an even shorter life, probably as short as a year or 20 months. We can only appreciate the ships of the past from various depictions in art, documents and models and attempts to reassemble fragments found in various excavations.

Initially, travel over coastal waters and nearby seas was the source of valuable food through fishing and extended hunting grounds. It also became an important factor in communications with other cultures and what we call 'community relations' today. Through colonisation you could extend your territory, your tribe and its status, your wealth and trade. It is easy to see the attraction of maritime life in this context and how seafaring leaders were revered and made into chiefs. We can also detect in this the origins of warfare at sea.

Shipbuilders gradually accumulated a vast knowledge of the materials available to them and their working characteristics. They built their ships initially to be navigated in local waters and then eventually to cross oceans, using the most basic navigational signals from the sky, sea and weather. They knew their subject and often tested their knowledge with unbelievable bravery.

The first requirement was buoyancy. A floating tree was a good start and wood was an obvious material to use. Where it was not available, there were often other growths that floated easily, such as reeds. Reed construction developed with large tightly bound bundles to build practical vessels. Animal skins were also used as a cladding for light branches shaped into hull forms. With fire and metal tools, suitable trees could be hollowed out to become the classic 'dug-out'. Ships of greater length and capacity became possible when tools were developed to split trees into planks. These could initially be used to add freeboard and extend the capabilities of the dug-out. When it became possible to attach them securely to each other, ships of greater length and capacity became achievable. Curved extensions fore and aft to form a bow and sternpost became practical. Location and purpose were critical to the type of vessel. Working in shallow waters, for example, needed quite a different approach to that required for the open sea.

THE INTRODUCTION OF SAIL

Early craft were probably propelled mostly by their crews. Poling led to rowing and an appreciation of the positive and negative effects of the wind. Exploiting the wind by hanging things up to catch it helped with propulsion. Animal hides extended on branches, woven reeds or early fabrics became sails as we know them today. The technologies relating to sail probably developed relatively quickly.

A single sail stretched from a yard hung from a mast was initially a 'fair wind' addition, used when the wind was coming from behind and of manageable strength. The sail was probably rectangular, the natural shape if one is using animal skins or household weaving sewn to maximise the area. Needing additional size for more extended sailing, more sails and more masts would be added. A topsail would be a modest addition to achieve greater mast height and start the long appreciation of the value of the slotting effect between sails.

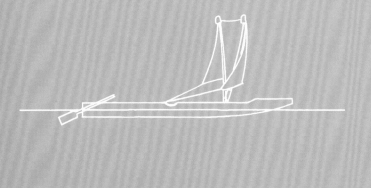

Dug-out Tree Boat
Man's first attempt at a sailing vessel perhaps two or three thousand years BC. Probably no more than ten metres long.

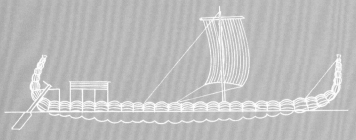

Reed Boat
Used in the Nile Delta and South America, including ocean crossings, from the earliest times mainly up to the middle ages, but still in use. Typically about 15 metres long.

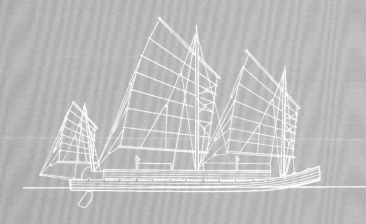

Bamboo Raft
Used from the earliest times in the South China Sea, with probably voyages further afield. Typically about 12 metres long.

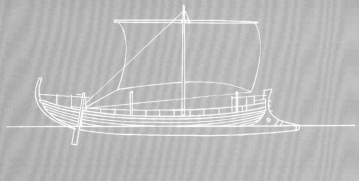

Greek Galley
Used from the earliest times throughout the Greek maritime area. Typically they might be 16 metres long.

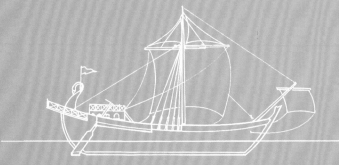

Roman Cargo Ship
Used throughout the first and second centuries AD, principally in the Mediterranean. Generally about 25 metres long.

The illustrations on this and page 19 are of typical sailing vessels that operated for periods of time from the earliest days of sail, up to a few centuries ago when the type of tall ships sailing today were introduced. All drawings © Colin Mudie

The effect of wind on a sail is complex. If the wind is more or less square on to it from behind, the result is, more or less, propulsion in that direction. If the wind comes at an angle, a whole range of effects develop, including 'lift', which allows a vessel to sail closer into the wind using the passage of air over the front as well as the back of the sail.

Hulls too are affected by being propelled at an angle through the water, as happens when the wind propulsion is not exactly in their direction. Unless this is controlled, hulls of almost any regular shape will just turn into the wind and drift. The introductions of the steering oar and, soon after, the rudder were spectacular advances. By steering the vessel and balancing the arrangements of sail, rig and hull, seamen could plan passages that included a recognisable windward element.

Wind is in itself a difficult force to contend with in terms of both direction and strength. It varies in reliability, sometimes blowing in regular patterns on which a seaman could depend, but often not. Unlike steamships, whose speed can be often determined by a lever connected to an engine and whose direction need take little account of the wind, a sailing vessel has to be worked in detail with the direction and strength of the available winds. The seafarer on a sailing vessel has to deal with whatever pressures the wind delivers, from the lightest of airs to the greatest and most destructive of tempests.

Varying the size and shape of sails was an early development. This led to the design of sail plans involving multiple sails and then an understanding of the interaction between them This became one of the most important skills of the sailor. It led to an appreciation of the value of setting sails as interrelated 'vanes' that increased the flow of air across the surfaces, resulting in more power. This development of power became increasingly valuable for the transport of heavy cargoes and for heavily armoured warships depending more and more on the ability to carry guns with speed and manoeuvrability.

LONG-DISTANCE VOYAGING

Archaeologists have found that the ancient artefacts discovered in the ports of antiquity were often sourced from many thousands of miles away across vast and sometimes turbulent oceans. Wood and metals, as well as other bulky and heavy cargoes, point to the use of quite substantial and seaworthy ships for the purpose of trading. There is evidence that long-distance voyaging on sailing ships began in a very small way a few thousand years ago. Indeed, virtually all international trade was conducted through the medium of sailing ships until the comparatively very recent inventions of the steamship, motor vehicle and aeroplane.

We are just beginning to appreciate how far the very early sailing craft travelled around the world. Thor Heyerdahl's research and voyaging indicates that very early mariners may have crossed the South Atlantic and penetrated deep into the Pacific using sail-driven rafts, journeying ever westward with little prospect of return.

The astonishing voyages of the Chinese Admiral Zheng He from 1405 to 1433 explored the seas all the way between China, Malaysia and the east coast of Africa, and possibly even further. What is totally extraordinary to us these days is that his fleets usually consisted of a few dozen very large treasure ships, eight-masted and more than 100 metres long, with hundreds of support vessels. Some confirmation of the size of his treasure ships has been the discovery of a rudderpost found near Nanking in 1962. It is not clear how his ships were built, but it may be that they were constructed using a whole selection of individual compartments possibly bolted together to form the watertight bulkheads and other features for which Chinese shipbuilding is renowned.

We are, of course, aware of the 15th-century western voyages of Columbus and Cabot across the Atlantic and they were possibly preceded by the Norsemen, Irishmen and others. The ships of that period were obviously up to seafaring in whatever conditions the oceans sent them. Long-distance voyaging opened up the world, with exploration recorded in detail by the science of chart making. Ships would go on exploratory voyages sometimes lasting years.

Two factors became important to the phenomenal growth in transocean voyaging: the development of aids to navigation and the size of the vessels themselves (determining capacity and influencing speed).

Viking Ship
The Vikings used their longships to invade much of Europe in the ninth and tenth centuries AD. They were open boats up to 35 metres long.

Dhow
The lateen rigged dhow was used in Arab waters, voyaging as far as China. Typically some 25 metres long.

Cog
The cog was a commonplace cargo ship from the 12th to the 14th century AD all over the Baltic, North Sea and into the Mediterranean. Generally about 20 metres long.

Chinese
The Chinese built ships of all sizes and sailed them from about the 14th century AD throughout the Pacific and as far as Africa. Their length ranged from about 30 metres up to 60 metres and sometimes longer.

Caravel
The square-rigged caravel redonda was used extensively in the 16th century AD and beyond for general use between Europe and Africa. They were generally about 25 metres long.

One of Chinese Admiral Zheng He's 'log roll' charts from the early 1400s
Photo: Admiral Zheng He Research Institute, China

THE DEVELOPMENT OF NAVIGATION TECHNOLOGIES

It is something of a mystery to this day how early sailors found their way over long distances across trackless waters. Of course, in the beginning it was largely done by sight and memory. If one sailed out of sight of one's home it was necessary to remember the visual references of the outward voyage and therefore the way home again. Exploring the seabed with sounding poles or lead weights on lengths of rope and recognising the prevailing winds and seas could help

with that. More importantly, there was observation of the sun and the moon and a myriad of identifiable stars at night when these were visible. Early navigation also benefited from a knowledge of quite esoteric subjects. The flights of birds and the areas where particular types of fish could be found were often as reliable indicators of location as anything else available to the mariner, as were the variations in wave patterns close to land and reefs or in open water.

From the earliest days the maritime world also relied on records of voyages. Successful routes would

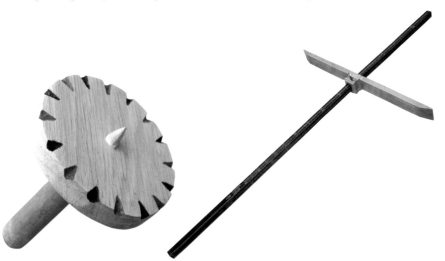

L–R: Sun compass, backstaff, astrolabe, octant, compass.
Photos: Max Mudie, and compass © Alex Staroseltsev via Shutterstock

sometimes be valuable secrets and only occasionally published. Charts and written voyage descriptions were developed into very reliable and often secret documents. An example might be the *periplus* or circumnavigations reported to the Persian king in the first century BC and restricted to his navy. Another would be the 'log roll' charts used by the Chinese Admiral Zheng He in the early 1400s.

The Vikings used crystals of Icelandic calcite to determine the location of the sun even in thick weather. Viking navigators often categorised the direction of the sun into times of day. This made a reliable directional reference in their northern latitudes where the sun was always low on the horizon. Other techniques are reputed to include the carriage of ravens. These, if released in open or thick conditions, either returned at once or made off on a direct run to the nearest land. The direction of the ravens' flight was a reliable aid to navigation. This incidentally is the technique reported for Noah when he discharged doves from the Ark to see if there was any land anywhere at all.

The compass was the first really useful mechanical aid to directional seagoing and was, and still is, a major aid to navigation. It was invented as a floating bar direction-indicator probably first by the Chinese from the magnetic lodestone, sometime between the first and second centuries BC. The lodestone was inserted in a block of wood floating in a bowl of water and one end pointed to the magnetic north. The interaction between the mariners of the great civilisations of around the first century undoubtedly meant that any such device would be widely used for voyaging between Africa, Arabia, India and China. They were surely used in the Mediterranean and probably spread north to some European navigators.

The first record of the compass being used in its modern, so-called dry form dates from 1321 near Naples, Italy. This took the form of a needle on a pivot in a bowl with a gimballed suspension to let it swing freely in a rolling and pitching ship. Somewhat later the gyrocompass was developed and then the whole range of modern equipment.

Telescopes and binoculars also became valuable aids to navigation when close to land. Optical instruments such as the octant, backstaff, astrolabe and sextant then developed to find a position from measurements relating to the sun and stars. Now, of course, all of these have been superseded by electronic systems such as radar and satellite navigation and electronic charts.

SHIP SIZE AND MATERIALS

Growth in the size and capacity of sailing ships, together with their improved seaworthiness and speed, essential for effective international trade and warfare, developed over more recent centuries. To begin with, size was directly related to available materials and tools to work them. Vessels constructed from reeds were usually short and those built of wood generally finished up with a practical maximum length of about 20 metres, due in large part to the length of available trees. Initially a tree also made a natural mast, but as ships grew bigger it was fairly normal to set one above the other in the form of topmasts to achieve greater height and available sail area. The tree was important, too, in relation to the yards from which sails were hung. Initially, the taller the tree the longer the yard on which a sail could be set.

Shipbuilders developed an increased understanding of the various qualities of different woods in terms of strength, stiffness and ease of shaping. It may be difficult for us, when we can just specify the timbers we want and accept them off a lorry, to realise what a close relationship there was between the wooden shipbuilders and their trees. It was commonplace for the builders to choose their timber while it was growing, and to know which growing locations were best for their purposes. The Greek galley builders of the third century BC, for example, specified species of trees grown on particular hillsides and such trees are still reserved for ship building today. Ships were planked with timbers matched port and starboard and with the bottom of the tree facing forward (where the wood is more dense and robust). Components also sometimes benefited from asymmetrical graining to maximise local strength. A considerable proportion of the structure of a wooden ship is curved. The face timbers often carry substantially stronger loadings than other sides and benefit from a closer grain pattern.

Before the onset of reliable metal fastenings, ships were assembled by skilled woodworkers using wood connections and joints to secure the structure. A plank might be attached to its neighbour by a series of wooden tongues individually secured with wooden pins. Other constructions used lashings to secure the skin planking and various materials were used to make them more watertight.

The arrival of metal fastenings transformed the construction of boats and ships. At its simplest it meant that planks could be fastened one to another in an overlapping style. The Vikings, with their open rowing-and-sailing craft used to roam the Atlantic and European waters, are a classic example of this. They initially still secured the ends of their planks to stem and stern by tucking them into recesses in the wood. The planks were secured one to another with short fastenings which were riveted (clenched) to fix them together (leading to the word 'clenched' as a description of a style of construction).

Such fastenings were at first made by the

builder, but the next major development came with the industrial manufacture of what we call bolts. This meant that the plank ends could be secured differently and the double ending of hulls was no longer such an attractive option. This, in turn, led to the development of rather round fat hulls that were much more suitable for transporting people, animals and other cargoes. Bolts could be used to support a wide range of building techniques and, among other characteristics, ships grew bigger. A key factor in this was that it allowed the joining of one length of stout timber to another to double the length of keel that could be used as the prime member of a new ship.

SAILS

Apart from its function of pure windage, anything exposed to the flow of wind is subject to what we now recognise as aerodynamics. The wind flow around any object produces variations in pressure. Our current familiarity with aircraft wings started, of course, with the simple single sheet sail. If such a sail is set at an angle to the wind flow the differences in wind flow between one side and another produces some element of suction which we now identify as lift. This aspect was discussed and illustrated earlier in this chapter on page 16 under 'the introduction of sail'. In its simplest form this helps a sail to act like a kite and pull in a direction other than straight downwind. With care and skill, this can drive a ship towards the wind, making windward ability a valuable characteristic of a rig. The modern Bermudan rig, the Arab dhow and schooner rigs are examples of such an ability. Square-rig, on the other hand, has attractions such as the development of sailing power and manoeuvrability to compensate for a modest reduction of windward ability.

Sails were probably made from whatever materials were available. The growth of ships brought a technical need for larger sails. Some, like the dhow, possibly to suit comparatively simple conditions, just increased the size of individual sails. The Europeans, with more complex winds, increased the numbers to allow quicker handling. The resulting 'square-rigger' developed a close interest in the relationships between individual small sails.

The push for bigger and bigger sailing ships was not without its constraints. One, of course, was the depth of water where a ship could travel or be berthed. Another, in the context of long-distance voyaging, was that initially they had no access to auxiliary power other than rowing. Relying on banks of oarsmen who needed to be both accommodated in numbers and fed for extended periods became impractical. This produced a total reliance on sail and in light winds these ships had very little windward ability. This was a serious problem, for instance, for ships trying to penetrate up rivers or across currents in a failing wind.

The ship designers responded to some of these constraints by increasing the sail area that could be set. It was one of the reasons for the development of multiple sails on several masts. This kept things within the ability of modest crew numbers to set and reduce total sail area as and when needed and was within the constraints of what was required to keep a mast upright and intact. As noted earlier, this also led to an appreciation that a stack of sails constituted a set of vanes which could interact with each other to increase the propulsion power substantially and improve a ship's ability to sail closer to the wind. Some shipmasters developed considerable skill in setting their available sail to optimise their power to suit every wind variation, and there are still some today who have that skill.

The tree was also of great value for masts and yards. To a certain extent, a mast firmly grounded in the hull needed very little extra support to carry a single sail. Trees are designed to bend and need very little support until the loads become heavy, and stretchy ropes gave adequate support in the early days. Only when rigs became complicated and masts spread to tiers of two, three or even four and the necessary support became complex did the need for strengthened and less flexible support coincide with the availability of metal wires. Latterly the use of such wire became more or less universal.

MORE RECENT DEVELOPMENTS

Mankind's use of the sea as a platform for travel has changed considerably over the past few centuries. From providing the opportunity for rather tentative voyages by relatively small ships, the oceans became major highways for international advancement, and ships grew to the largest practical sizes for wood construction and wind power. The technologies developed with the specific demands for specialist ships to traverse the oceans, often in competition, for commerce, warfare and adventure. The design of warships, in particular, developed to accommodate the conflicting requirements of speed, manoeuvrability and the need to carry the greatest numbers of cannons. Cargo ships developed in size to accommodate bulk cargoes, with rigs to allow them to be handled by the minimum number of expensive crew.

The 18th and 19th centuries produced a spectacular degree of maritime activity and this was almost totally by ships with only the most marginal of power other than the winds and currents to help them. This might include the use of their boats and

anchors and sometimes oarsmen, but these were not of much help in most voyaging. The pressures of warfare and commerce drove the design of sailing ships to a very high degree of sophistication.

All over the world sailing ships developed to suit local conditions. In the Western world, the bigger ships ranged between two extreme types. Warships were planned to be short and fat with great stability to carry very heavy loads of guns and crews which might run to 1,000 men and their supplies for several months. These were maritime castles and needed the maximum stability to be able to fire their guns, especially those through open ports close to the waterline. Such warships set large sails quickly and efficiently, thanks to their large crews, and set them with the greatest efficiency for optimum performance in battle.

At the other end of the spectrum, a spectacular development came from the financial rewards from making the fastest delivery of the latest crop

Second Battle of Virginia Capes by V Zveg. Sourced from Wikimedia Commons

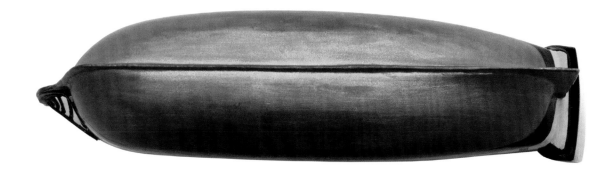

of Chinese tea to the Western capitals in the 19th century. This involved lightweight cargoes on board the fastest sailing ships capable of racing halfway around the world. This attracted the designers, builders and especially racing captains to develop large, long, light, sharp-ended ships rigged with a magnificent outfit of sails. These ships were renowned for their special ability to 'clip' along and this is where the evocative word 'clipper' comes from. Their development went about as far as might be envisaged before steam took over with the ability to power through the windless parts of the voyage and to motor through the Suez and Panama canals.

As metal technology advanced it was often used for the difficult and time-consuming items of wood construction. Initially it was framing, which could be planked with wood, and eventually it was the whole ship, with wood relegated to decking and furnishing. Eventually even the masts and spars were made of steel tubing. Latterly aluminium was chosen for such rigging items.

With the use of iron and steel, the constructional constraints of size disappeared. Some sizeable sailing ships were built and put into service. The problems of operating such ships in and out of port were largely overcome by the use of radio to arrange tugs as required.

Voyages between continents lasted for three or four months. Sailing ships were seen as such reliable conveyances that worldwide travel for people and goods became commonplace in the 19th century. There were, of course, wrecks and disappearances, but world travel involved thousands of sailing ships of all sizes, including some up to several thousands of tons. International communications became the norm.

The steel steam or diesel ship supported by radio more or less took over the maritime industry in the last century. With the arrival of the steam engine, sail was

The American clipper ship Flying Cloud *at sea under full sail* by Antonio Jacobsen. Sourced from Wikimedia Commons

Hull models (above and opposite): Colin Mudie. **Photos**: Max Mudie

relegated largely to the picturesque, to the romantic adventurer and sporting sailor and to the activity and purposes of sail training described in Chapter Three.

There have been several attempts to apply our latest technologies to use wind as auxiliary propulsion to reduce fuel costs. The major problem is that sails and their rig are bulky, which is not a problem at sea but quite often interferes with cargo and passenger handling in port – currently a major cost item in any commercial voyage. It also involves manpower with specific skills. Several attempts have been made to reintroduce a combination of modern sails with auxiliary engines. Some have used rotating vertical cylinders for wind propulsion. A current proposition is to fully integrate the development of power from all the sources accessible to a ship at sea – wind, solar power and diesel generators, etc. – and this may be a way forward.

THE FUTURE

There are several projects planned, some already at sea, to advance the use of sail with modern materials such as carbon fibre, plastics, etc. There is also considerable interest in using the power available on board to replace manual handling of sails and ropes, and even to control these things by computer so that

a ship of any size could be sailed from a single panel.

One way to overcome the size problem would be by adding power-assist as and when required from a combination of diesel generators and batteries, which would also be fed from photo-voltaic sails. In addition to assisting operations at sea, this would enable the ship to be largely self-contained for harbour manoeuvring, with the aid, of course, of azimuth thrusters.

The rig of a future ship could be set on mast towers which would leave the deck area free for other activities. This system of towers would also enable the rig to be changed simply and easily in a matter of hours if required. Preference would be as a

barque, currently the favourite for sail training. On-board accommodation would be modular and easily assembled and disassembled to enable the ship to be used for a wide variety of purposes and clientele, from sail trainers to VIPs. The 200-metre barque pictured below could incorporate many of these possibilities.

Other more technologically adventurous sailing ships are on various drawing boards around the world. But these innovative designers will surely also have to remember that it will all come down to who will man them. For thousands of years the seaman has been the principal factor in the development of ships. This factor will not change, at least not in the foreseeable future.

© Colin Mudie

THE TALL SHIPS

THE GLAMOUR AND DIVERSITY OF TALL SHIPS SAILING TODAY

MICHAEL RAUWORTH (INTRODUCTION) AND NIGEL ROWE (THE SHIPS)

2

Photo: Statsraad Lehmkuhl Foundation

INTRODUCTION

Before the Industrial Revolution brought forth railroads, steamships, mechanised factories and the like, the sailing ship was arguably the most sophisticated creation of mankind. Today, though, many view the sailing ship as anachronistic. True, tall ships are magic for the eye. They seize people's attention, draw crowds, energise the news media and inspire floods of photos, not to mention an abundance of artwork back through history. But these things alone cannot account for why we have such ships today. The answer to this, though, is not such a mystery.

Sailing ships are obviously not part of the modern industrial infrastructure. But three important values have kept them in the public eye nevertheless. One is their historical importance and their value in preserving a nation's maritime heritage, often as stationary museum ships and tourist attractions. In this they share a kinship with the preservation of historic buildings ashore. At the other end of the spectrum is the recent exploration of modern-day wind-power devices to supplement the diesel power of modern-day industrial vessels – for both economic and environmental reasons.

But as sailing ships faded from commerce, the importance – to seafarers – of the experience on these ships still remained; this is the second value. Military fleets and the merchant shipping industry were the first to take advantage of this. They retained or acquired existing sailing ships or built new ones, to be at the core of their training programme for officer cadets. The professional seafaring skills the cadets learned on a tall ship were vital, of course. But this challenging experience also made for important individual character development – courage, self-confidence, teamwork, leadership and other important interpersonal qualities. These qualities were soon seen as empowering for young people generally in the wider community. These aspects are explored thoroughly in the next chapter, *The Tall Ship Experience*. But the value of sail training is manifest in this chapter, too. All of the ships featured are active at sea today. While a number of them also undertake charter and passenger work, they all conduct sail training programmes and for most of them this is their sole purpose.

The collection of ships in this chapter consists mostly of vessels with what are known as 'traditional rigs', namely square-riggers and gaff-riggers. Many of the ships featured began life as industrial vessels serving the economy of earlier times and have been restored, improved or adapted to serve the modern purpose of sail training. An example is *Kruzenshtern* (Russia), which began life carrying cargoes of saltpetre from South America to northern Europe and today cruises the world as a training platform for Russian maritime cadets. Another is *Creoula* (Portugal), which began life as a fishing schooner and now combines research work with sail training programmes. *Adventuress* (USA) was built for a research expedition a century ago and now combines marine observations with sail training programmes.

Replica vessels share many characteristics with the restored vessels. Sometimes they are built as near-recreations of specific vessels. In other cases, they represent a respected type or class of vessel from the past. Quite often they make extensive use of the materials and methods of the historic period they evoke, even though they are typically fitted with appropriate modern safety equipment. In any event, just as with the restored vessels, they evoke the public's appreciation for the history that the original ship embodied. Examples of this type include *Albanus* (Finland), *Götheborg* (Sweden), *Lady Washington* (USA), *Shtandart* (Russia), *Spirit of Bermuda* (Bermuda) and *Vera Cruz* (Portugal). In fact, *Shtandart* was built at the end of the last century using the materials, tools and techniques to hand in the early 1700s. *Götheborg* is the world's largest operational wooden sailing vessel, launched in 2003. The original *Götheborg* was owned by the Swedish East India Company and was returning from China in 1745 heavily laden with tea, porcelain and silver when she ran aground and sank just outside her home port of Gothenburg.

PROFESSIONALISM IN SEAFARING

Professionalism in seafaring has been another major force, as noted earlier. Since the advent of steamships, the elders of seamanship held that experience at sea under sail was especially valuable for anyone who aspired to be master of a ship of any kind, including the increasing fleet of steamships that grew to dominate world trade, later to be overtaken themselves by diesel-powered ships.

For many years, aspiring steamship officers could find this experience of 'intense seafaring' by securing a position, sometimes as an apprentice, on board one of the surviving sailing ships that were then still active in carrying cargo. But the first half of the 1900s saw a new phenomenon in this vein: ships with little or no cargo capacity that were instead designed and built from the keel up for the fundamental purpose of training young people under sail, for a career as an officer of a seagoing service. In these ships, then, the objective of professional seafaring training was not a secondary objective to the business of carrying cargo. This movement is well illustrated in today's fleet by examples such as *Amerigo Vespucci* (Italy), *Juan Sebastián de Elcano* (Spain) and by three existing training ships built

as sisters in the 1930s: *Mircea* (Romania), *Sagres* (Portugal) and *Eagle* (USA).

It will come as no surprise that ships of this kind are commonly built and operated by national governments, maritime universities and schools. Officers trained aboard these vessels are expected to pursue vocations in one of several types of seafaring – the cargo-carrying fleet of the nation's merchant marine, its fleet of fishing vessels, its military navy and coastguard. More than this, these ships have also become seagoing ambassadors for their home nations, a splendid tool for spreading international goodwill and building national pride. Little wonder then that the building of dedicated sea-officer vocational training ships did not stop in the 1930s. South America and Europe are home to ships in this book that are good examples of this: *Libertad* (Argentina), *Cisne Branco* (Brazil), *Esmeralda* (Chile), *Dar Młodzieży* (Poland) and *Mir* (Russia). In more recent years, tall ship building has expanded yet further in a number of other countries. Examples include India, with the launch of *Sudarshini* in 2012 to join *Tarangini* as a navy training ship, and the Sultanate of Oman with a new tall ship modelled on the Dutch *Stad Amsterdam* due to enter service in 2015 to train officer cadets for the country's navy, succeeding the *Shabab Oman*.

The harvest of personal qualities from a sailing ship experience was valuable for more than a career at sea. This led the international tall ships fleet to expand to reach deliberately non-vocational purposes, and this is the third major value. Together with other advocates of experiential learning, the Australian Alan Villiers and the American Irving Johnson are widely recognised as pioneers in this phenomenon. Each went to sea on a deep-sea sailing ship and then put together voyages for young people designed to use the sea experience as training for life rather than for a career at sea. Their work in the 1930s–1950s served as the foundation for a major part of today's tall ship fleet.

This category of ships enables their trainees to be integrated fully in the working of the vessel. Trainees stand watches around the clock at the helm, on lookout and the like, take on galley and cleaning chores, handle sail aloft and on deck and assist with repair and maintenance work, alongside the vessel's professional crew. They are absorbed into an environment of seafaring professionalism and expected to perform accordingly – with due recognition of their 'newcomer' status. While aboard, they are placed into close engagement with the sea, its enchantment and its peril. Many count the challenges they meet on board a sailing ship as a major turning point in their lives.

NON-VOCATIONAL MISSION

This non-vocational sail training mission involves vessels that have been specifically built for this purpose. Examples include *Fryderyk Chopin* (Poland), *Christian Radich* (Norway), *Exy Johnson* (USA), *Alexander von Humboldt II* (Germany); historic vessels put to this service such as *Jolie Brise* (UK) and *Jens Krogh* (Denmark); vessels built as replicas such as *Shtandart* (Russia), *Pride of Baltimore II*, *Niagara* (both USA) and *Lady Nelson* (Australia); and vessels that have been modified from hulls originally built for another service converted to sail training, including *De Gallant* (Netherlands), *Picton Castle* (Cook Islands) and *Roald Amundsen* (Germany).

Other influences play a role, too. Some sailing ships make certain voyages carrying individuals as passengers in the classic (non-working) sense, such as *Stad Amsterdam* (Netherlands). *Picton Castle* (Cook Islands) makes periodic circumnavigations with

trainees and some passengers. Others are dedicated to a special focus, such as scouting on *Zawisza Czarny II* (Poland) or the disabled on *Lord Nelson* and *Tenacious* (both UK). HM *Bark Endeavour* (Australia) tours mainly as a 'living museum'. A number of vessels have environmental research and education as a major factor in their mission or programme. Examples of this are *Tre Kronor af Stockholm* (Sweden), *Brabander* (Lithuania) and *Corwith Cramer* (USA). Still others combine several of the above purposes, such as *Santa Maria Manuela* (Portugal).

The more than 100 ships illustrated in this chapter wear the flags of some 36 nations, and their origins date back as far as the 1870s. Individually focused sail training and sea-officer vocational training account for the great bulk of their work, but there is a considerable range of nuance in their occupation. Their voyages vary widely from day trips and week-long voyages to semester-long educational programmes and year-long circumnavigations.

This short introduction gives a flavour only of what is to be found in the following 130 pages, with write-ups on each ship by Nigel Rowe and some spectacular photographs contributed by more than 100 photographers from around the world. Although small in tonnage compared with the world's commercial and military fleets, the tall ship fleet stands apart. They are – uniquely – the product of benevolent objectives, and perhaps for that reason are particularly deserving of the special attention they attract.

Photo: Max Mudie

THE SHIPS

SHIP RIGS

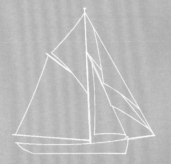

Gaff Cutter

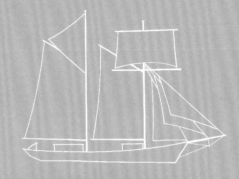

Two Mast Topsail Schooner

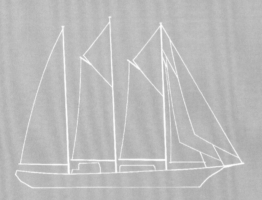

Three Mast Schooner

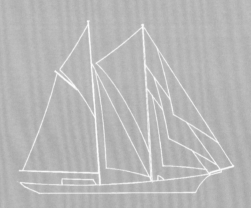

Two Mast Staysail Schooner

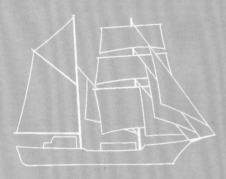

Brigantine

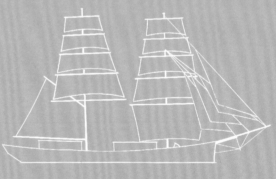

Brig

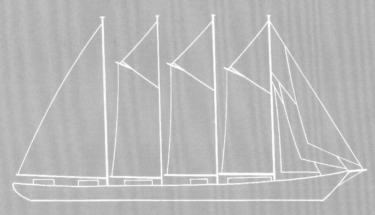

Four Mast Schooner

Three Mast Barquentine

Three Mast Barque

Full Rigged Ship

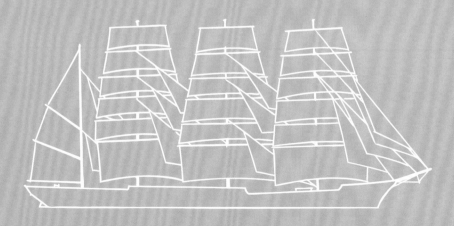

Four Mast Barque

Adventuress

Adventuress is one of only two National Historic Landmark sailing ships still operating on the west coast of the USA. Launched in 1913, she was built for the owner of the Chicago Yellow Cab Company for an Arctic expedition by the American Museum of Natural History. On board was the naturalist Roy Chapman Andrews who later discovered fossilised dinosaur eggs in Mongolia and served as the inspiration for Hollywood's Indiana Jones. Now owned by the non-profit Sound Experience, she is a Pacific Northwest icon providing thousands of people every year with an opportunity to sail the ship and participate in marine environmental observations and other projects.

Photos: (below) Adventuress Archive, (below right) Elizabeth T Becker

National flag	USA
Home port	Seattle
Sparred length	40.54 m
Rig	Schooner
Sail area	508.9 sq m
Gross tons	98
Hull material	Wood (oak, purple heart, sapele)
Owner/operator	Sound Experience
Built	East Boothbay, Maine
Launched	1913

W www.soundexp.org **E** mail@soundexp.org

Albanus

This replica of a 1908 Finnish freighter called *Albanus* is a traditional Finnish sailing vessel built of local pine in the Åland Islands. A two-masted schooner (*galeas* in Finnish), she was launched in Mariehamn in 1988 and is owned and operated by the Ship Association Albanus. *Albanus* is used mainly as a sail training vessel for schools and other youth groups, but also undertakes a variety of charter work in the archipelagoes of Åland and Åboland.

Photos: Albanus Archive

National flag	Åland Islands, Finland
Home port	Mariehamn
Sparred length	30 m
Rig	Schooner
Sail area	303 sq m
Gross tons	80
Hull material	Wood (pine)
Owner/operator	Skeppsföreningen Albanus
Built	Mariehamn, Finland
Launched	1988

W www.aland.net/albanus E albanus@aland.net

Alexander von Humboldt II

Launched in 2011, the *Alexander von Humboldt II* is one of the most modern tall ships afloat in terms of both design and on-board equipment. She was designed for the exclusive purpose of sail training by the German Sail Training Federation (DSST), reflecting the organisation's long experience with her predecessor, *Alexander von Humboldt*, a converted lightship built in 1906. The *Alexander von Humboldt II* operates throughout the year with an all-volunteer crew, sailing in the North Sea and Baltic during the summer months and in the Mediterranean, the Canaries and the Cape Verde Islands during the winter, with occasional voyages across the Atlantic to the Caribbean and South America.

Photos: Maurizio Gambarini

National flag	Germany
Home port	Bremerhaven
Sparred length	65 m
Rig	Barque
Sail area	1,350 sq m
Gross tons	763
Hull material	Welded steel
Owner/operator	Deutsche Stiftung Sail Training (DSST)
Built	Bremen and Bremerhaven, Germany
Launched	2011

W www.alex-2.de **E** info@alex-2.de

Amerigo Vespucci

Amerigo Vespucci was one of two school ships ordered in 1925 by the Royal Italian Navy. The design of both was inspired by large 18th-century 74-cannon warships. The first of the two to be built, *Cristoforo Colombo*, was taken by the Soviet Union as war reparations after World War II and decommissioned soon afterwards. Meanwhile, *Amerigo Vespucci* has continued to sail as a training ship for Italian Navy cadets, mostly in European waters, but occasionally further afield. She completed a circumnavigation in 2002.

Photos: Cinefoto – Marina Militare Italiana

National flag	Italy
Home port	La Spezia
Sparred length	101 m
Rig	Full-rigged ship
Sail area	1,700 sq m
Displacement	4,146 tons
Hull material	Steel
Owner/operator	Italian Navy
Built	Naples, Italy
Launched	1931

W www.marina.difesa.it/uominimezzi/navi/Pagine/Vespucci.aspx **E** vespucci@marina.difesa.it

HM Bark Endeavour

This replica of James Cook's famous ship is the product of meticulous research to ensure authenticity but with hidden facilities and equipment to comply with modern requirements of safety and comfort. The original *Endeavour* was a Whitby collier, converted by the British Admiralty to enable Cook's great maritime adventures and discoveries in 1769–1771, including the charting of eastern Australia. The replica *Endeavour* was launched in 1993. She has completed two circumnavigations, but her principal mission is as a 'living museum', visiting ports around Australia as well as her home base in Sydney to demonstrate 18th-century seafaring and shipboard life.

Photos: Australian National Maritime Museum

National flag	Australia
Home port	Sydney
Sparred length	43.7 m
Rig	Full-rigged ship
Sail area	930 sq m
Gross tons	397
Hull material	Wood (jarrah and oregon)
Owner/operator	Australian National Maritime Museum
Built	Fremantle, Western Australia
Launched	1993
W www.anmm.gov.au/endeavour	
E endeavour@anmm.gov.au	

Belem

The three-masted barque *Belem* is the last of the 19th-century French trading ships still under sail and has had an extraordinary career. Built at Chantenay-sur-Loire, near Nantes, and launched in 1896, she was originally a cargo ship. She was sold in 1914 to the Duke of Westminster who converted her to a luxurious private yacht sailing under the British flag. In 1922, she was acquired by Sir Arthur Guinness who sailed her extensively, including a circumnavigation with his two daughters. *Belem* was sold in 1949, after Sir Arthur's death, to Count Vittorio Cini of Venice who rerigged her as a barquentine to serve as a sail training ship under the Italian flag, which she did until the mid 1960s. She was then moored at an island off Venice until she was finally brought back to France in 1979 and restored to her original condition. She now sails under the French flag again as a sail training ship.

Photos: (below) Yann Mengy, (below right) Benjamin Decoin

National flag	France
Home port	Nantes
Sparred length	58 m
Rig	Barque
Sail area	1,200 sq m
Displacement	800 tons
Hull material	Riveted steel
Owner/operator	The Belem Foundation
Built	Chantenay-sur-Loire, France
Launched	1896

W www.fondationbelem.com
E contact@fondationbelem.fr

Belle Poule, Etoile and Mutin

The French Navy has a strong tradition of sail training for its officer cadets. *Belle Poule* and *Etoile* were built in 1932 as twins to a design based on the very seaworthy Icelandic fishing vessels of the early 1900s. During World War II both vessels were used to train sailors for the Free French Navy. The design of *Mutin* is similar to the tuna-fishing vessels of the late 1800s. She was built in 1927 for pilotage training and is now the oldest vessel in the service of the French Navy. She was commandeered during World War II by the British Special Operations Executive and used for espionage missions and related purposes in the Atlantic and Mediterranean. In addition to training navy cadets, all three vessels serve today as ambassadors for French maritime and cultural interests.

Belle Poule (BP), Etoile (E), Mutin (M)	
National flag	France
Home port	Brest
Sparred length	37.50 m (BP, E), 33 m (M)
Rig	Topsail schooner (BP, E), Topsail yawl (M)
Sail area	450 sq m (BP, E), 350 sq m (M)
Gross tons	275 (BP, E), 67 (M)
Hull material	Wood (oak)
Owner/operator	French Navy
Built	Fécamp, France (BP, E), Les Sables d'Olonne, France (M)
Launched	1932 (BP, E), 1927 (M)
W www.ecole-navale.fr **E** activites-voiliers@ecole-navale.fr	

Photos: (right) Marine Nationale – Julie Barthel

Opposite page: (top left) Marine Nationale – Johann Pesche
(top right) Marine Nationale – Alain Monot
(bottom) Marine Nationale – Johann Pesche

Brabander

Brabander was built in the 1970s in the Netherlands to serve as a sailing school ship and takes her name from the Dutch region where she was built. She was acquired in 2006 by the University of Klaipėda in Lithuania and underwent a number of modifications to equip her for a wide range of purposes, including conventional sail training programmes for the university's students and others and marine research in fields such as hydrography, ornithology and underwater archaeology and geology. She also represents Lithuania at a number of national and international maritime events in the Baltic and beyond.

Photos: Klaipėda University

National flag	Lithuania
Home port	Klaipėda, Lithuania
Sparred length	36 m
Rig	Gaff-rigged topsail schooner
Sail area	440 sq m
Gross tons	100
Hull material	Steel
Owner/operator	Klaipėda University
Built	Drimmelen, Netherlands
Launched	1977

W www.ku.lt/en/fleet/sv-brabander/
E valdemaras.vizbaras@ku.lt

Christian Radich

Christian Radich was built in 1937 in Norway and sailed as a school ship until 1998, giving almost 17,000 young Norwegians their basic marine education. The ship is known worldwide from her starring roles in the movie *Windjammer* (1958) and the TV series *The Onedin Line* (1971–1980). During the summer season, *Christian Radich* provides sail training voyages for individuals and groups. She has participated in tall ships races since the first such regatta in 1956, and has won more races than any of her keen competitors. During the winter months in the northern hemisphere, she is used for Norwegian Navy training programmes and is occasionally available to civilians for midwinter voyages in southern Europe and across the Atlantic.

Photos: (below) Leif Brestrup, (below right) Christian Radich Archive

National flag	Norway
Home port	Oslo
Sparred length	73 m
Rig	Full-rigged ship
Sail area	1,360 sq m
Gross tons	663
Hull material	Riveted steel
Owner/operator	Stiftelsen Skoleskipet Christian Radich
Built	Sandefjord, Norway
Launched	1937
W www.radich.no **E** postmaster@radich.no	

Cisne Branco

Cisne Branco (White Swan) was launched in 2000, just in time for her maiden voyage across the Atlantic from Amsterdam to celebrate the 500th anniversary of the discovery of Brazil by the Portuguese Admiral Pedro Álvares Cabral. She is a sister to the Dutch ship *Stad Amsterdam*. *Cisne Branco* serves as an international ambassador for Brazil, promoting the country and its culture, and as a training ship for military cadets. She is the third Brazilian Navy sail training ship to be called *Cisne Branco*. The name derives from a Brazilian song called 'Ballad of the Seaman', whose lyrics liken a sailing ship to a white swan.

National flag	Brazil
Home port	Rio de Janeiro
Sparred length	76 m
Rig	Full-rigged ship
Sail area	2,195 sq m
Gross tons	698
Hull material	Steel
Owner/operator	Brazilian Navy
Built	Gorinchem, Netherlands
Launched	2000

W www.mar.mil.br **E** rpcisnebranco@gmail.com

Photos: (right) Brazilian Navy

Opposite page: (top) Thad Koza
(bottom) Brazilian Navy

Corwith Cramer and Robert C Seamans

These ships were named after the founding director (Corwith Cramer) and a former chairman (Robert C Seamans) of the Sea Education Association (SEA). Both were built as oceanographic research vessels for operation under sail and are certified by the US Coast Guard as sailing school vessels. The *Robert C Seamans* is the most sophisticated ship of her kind ever built in the USA. The SEA organisation was established in 1971 to give undergraduate students the opportunity to study the ocean from the platform of a traditional sailing ship. Its vessels have sailed more than one million nautical miles and educated more than 7,500 students.

Corwith Cramer (CC), Robert C Seamans (RCS)	
National flag	USA
Home port	Woods Hole, Massachusetts
Sparred length	40.8 m (CC), 41 m (RCS)
Rig	Brigantine
Sail area	697 sq m (CC), 795 sq m (RCS)
Gross tons	158 (CC), 211 (RCS)
Hull material	Steel
Owner/operator	Sea Education Association (SEA)
Built	Bilbao, Spain (CC), Tacoma, USA (RCS)
Launched	1987 (CC), 2001 (RCS)

W www.sea.edu E admission@sea.edu

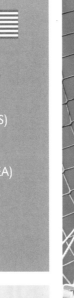

Photos: Sea Education Association

Creoula

Built in 1937 as one of the great Portuguese White Fleet schooners for fishing cod on the Grand Banks of Nova Scotia, *Creoula* was acquired in 1979 by the Portuguese Ministry of Fisheries and Agriculture to become a fisheries museum. However, her hull was in such good condition that she underwent a major refurbishment instead.

She was then transferred to the Ministry of Defence to serve mainly as a sail training ship and as ambassador for Portuguese maritime affairs. She has also undertaken a number of scientific expeditions. Since the late 1980s, *Creoula* has covered more than 100,000 nautical miles and 16,000 people have sailed on her.

Photos: Portuguese Navy

National flag	Portugal
Home port	Lisbon
Sparred length	67.4 m
Rig	Schooner
Sail area	1,244 sq m
Gross tons	1,300
Hull material	Steel
Owner/operator	Portuguese Ministry of Defence
Built	Lisbon, Portugal
Launched	1937
W www.marinha.pt/pt-pt/servicos/ntm-creoula	
E creoula@marinha.pt	

Cuauhtémoc

Owned and operated by the Mexican Navy as a sailing school ship, *Cuauhtémoc* is named after the last Aztec emperor. She acts as an international 'sailing ambassador' for her country and has covered more than 400,000 nautical miles since her launch in 1982. *Cuauhtémoc* is the last of four windjammers built by shipyards in Bilbao, Spain, for Latin American navies; the others are *Gloria* (Colombia), *Guayas* (Ecuador) and *Simón Bolívar* (Venezuela).

Photos: Max Mudie

National flag	Mexico
Home port	Acapulco
Sparred length	90.50 m
Rig	Barque
Sail area	2,200 sq m
Displacement	1,800 tons
Hull material	Steel
Owner/operator	Mexican Navy
Built	Bilbao, Spain
Launched	1982

Danmark

Built in the Danish port of Nakskov as a sail training ship, the *Danmark* continues to provide basic training for young men and women aged 17½–23 seeking a career at sea. Today, the 20-week training programme to become an ordinary seaman includes 14 weeks of sailing on the *Danmark*, with 80 students per course. The on-board language is English as trainees are recruited from throughout the European Union. The training generally takes place in European waters.

National flag	Denmark
Home port	Copenhagen
Sparred length	74.4 m
Rig	Full-rigged ship
Sail area	1,638 sq m
Gross tons	737
Hull material	Steel
Owner/operator	Danish government/Martec
Built	Nakskov, Denmark
Launched	1933

W www.martec.nu **E** martec@martec.nu

Photos: (right) Ebbe Kyrø

Opposite page: (top left) Finn Føns
(top right) Ebbe Kyrø
(bottom) Niels Nyholm

Dar Młodzieży

Dar Młodzieży (Gift of Youth) was built in 1982 as a training ship for Gdynia Maritime University in Poland – a successor to the old frigate *Dar Pomorza* (now a museum ship). *Dar Młodzieży* is the prototype of a series of six frigates built in Gdansk Shipyard in Poland, the other five having been ordered by maritime schools in the former Soviet Union. The ship is now used by students of Gdynia and Szczecin Maritime Universities, as well as those of other institutions outside Poland. She has undertaken many extended voyages, including a circumnavigation, clocking up more than half a million nautical miles and training more than 15,000 merchant navy cadets.

National flag	Poland
Home port	Gdynia
Sparred length	108.8 m
Rig	Full-rigged ship
Sail area	3,015 sq m
Gross tons	2,255
Hull material	Steel
Owner/operator	Gdynia Maritime University
Built	Gdansk, Poland
Launched	1982
W www.am.gdynia.pl **E** pror3@am.gdynia.pl	

Photos: Maciej Stobierski

De Gallant

Built in the Netherlands in 1916 as a herring drifter, *De Gallant* had several owners and names before being acquired by her current owners. She was sold in the late 1920s to a Danish company that installed an engine and used her for cargo work. She was then sold to a Swedish company before returning to the Netherlands in 1981. In the hands of her current owners she underwent a major restoration and rebuild from 1986 to 1993 as part of a work-experience programme for disadvantaged young people. Since then she has sailed mainly in the North Atlantic, North Sea and Baltic as a sail training vessel for young people.

Photos: (below) De Gallant Archive, (below right) Martin Blouet

National flag	Netherlands
Home port	Amsterdam
Sparred length	36 m
Rig	Gaff schooner
Sail area	400 sq m
Gross tons	88
Hull material	Steel
Owner/operator	Stichting Zeilschip de Gallant/ Hendrik de Roo
Built	Vlaardingen, Netherlands
Launched	1916

W www.degallant.nl **E** gallant@xs4all.nl

KRI Dewaruci

Although launched in 1953, work began on *Dewaruci* for the Indonesian Navy some 20 years earlier at a shipyard in Hamburg, Germany. Work was suspended at the outbreak of World War II during which the yard was heavily damaged, requiring major reconstruction.

The ship was finally completed in 1952 and launched the following year, since when she has served as a training ship for naval cadets and a goodwill ambassador for Indonesia. Her name is drawn from Indonesian legend, Dewaruci being the 'ruler and guardian of the sea'.

Photos: (below) Herbert H Boehm, (below right) Max Mudie

National flag	Indonesia
Home port	Surabaya
Sparred length	58.3 m
Rig	Barquentine
Sail area	1,100 sq m
Gross tons	847
Hull material	Steel
Owner/operator	Indonesian Navy
Built	Hamburg, Germany
Launched	1953
E info@kridewaruci.com	

USCG Eagle

Built in Germany in 1936, the US Coast Guard barque *Eagle* was included in reparations paid to the United States following World War II. Since 1946, the Coast Guard has used her as a training vessel for future officers. Some 750–850 cadets are trained every year on *Eagle*, and for many it is their first taste of life at sea. *Eagle* generally sails in the waters along the US East and West Coasts and around the Caribbean, with occasional voyages to Europe and elsewhere in the world. As the US government's only active square-rigger, she often serves an ambassadorial role on visits to foreign ports.

National flag	USA
Home port	New London, Connecticut
Sparred length	89.9 m
Rig	Barque
Sail area	2,072 sq m
Gross tons	1,842
Hull material	Steel
Owner/operator	United States Coast Guard (USCG)
Built	Hamburg, Germany
Launched	1936 (commissioned into USCG 1946)
W www.cga.edu/eagle	

Photos: US Coast Guard

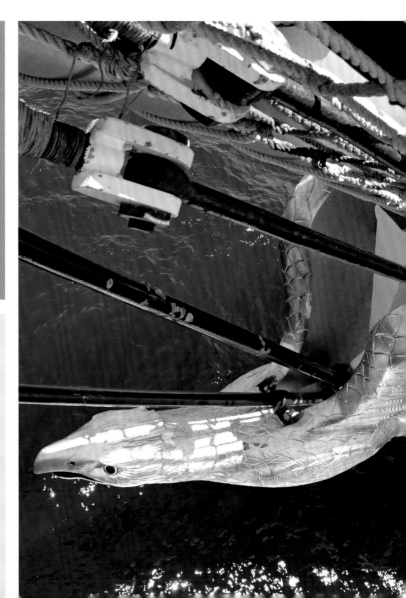

Eendracht

Although *Eendracht* was not built until 1989, her heritage dates back to 1938 when a national association was created in the Netherlands to promote traditional maritime skills. From this organisation a foundation, today known as Stichting Zeilschip Eendracht, was established to facilitate the building of a sail training ship. *Eendracht* was launched by Her Majesty Queen Beatrix in 1989. Her main focus is on sail training, and trainees up to the age of 25 can benefit from the foundation's bursary fund.

Photos: Max Mudie

National flag	Netherlands
Home port	Rotterdam
Sparred length	59.08 m
Rig	Schooner
Sail area	1,206 sq m
Gross tons	606
Hull material	Steel
Owner/operator	Stichting Zeilschip Eendracht
Built	Gorinchem, Netherlands
Launched	1989

W www.eendracht.nl **E** info@eendracht.nl

Esmeralda

Construction began on the *Esmeralda* in 1946. Originally intended to be a sail training ship for the Spanish Navy, her completion was delayed and she was not launched until 1953. By that time Spain had agreed to transfer ownership of the ship to Chile in recognition of debts incurred during the Spanish Civil War. Since then *Esmeralda* has had a distinguished career as the Chilean Navy's sail training tall ship and floating ambassador, sailing 1.2 million nautical miles and training 7,000 cadets. She has visited some 200 ports in more than 70 countries.

Photos: Thad Koza

National flag	Chile
Home port	Valparaíso
Sparred length	113 m
Rig	Barquentine
Sail area	2,870 sq m
Displacement	3,673 tons
Hull material	Steel
Owner/operator	Chilean Navy
Built	Cádiz, Spain
Launched	1953

W www.esmeralda.cl **E** esmeralda@skyfile.com

Europa

Europa was built in 1911 and served as a lightship for the German Federal Coast Guard until 1977. Several years later she was acquired by Dutch owners and underwent a major rebuild and modification to convert her to the traditional three-masted barque she is today. She has an unusual sail plan with a total of 30 sails, including six studding sails. *Europa* sails throughout the year as a sail training ship for people of all ages and nationalities. Her adventurous global sailing programme includes annual voyages to the Antarctic and occasional circumnavigations, as well as sailing and racing in European waters.

National flag	Netherlands
Home port	The Hague
Sparred length	56 m
Rig	3 Barque
Sail area	1,250 sq m
Gross tonnage	303
Hull material	Riveted steel
Owner/operator	Reederij Bark EUROPA
Launched	1911 (rebuilt and relaunched 1994)

W www.barkeuropa.com **E** info@barkeuropa.com

Photos: (right) M&A Edixhoven

Opposite page: (top left) Jordi Plana
(top right) Helen Keep
(bottom) Hajo Olij

Exy Johnson and Irving Johnson

These two ships are identical twins, built at the same time in Los Angeles and launched in 2002. They take their name from Exy (Electa) and Irving Johnson, an American couple who pioneered adventure sail training in the 1930s–1950s. During this time, they completed seven circumnavigations in two 30-metre converted pilot schooners (both called *Yankee*), each time with a crew of 20 young men and women. *Exy Johnson* and *Irving Johnson* serve as sail training vessels, mostly for young people in the Los Angeles area, with a focus on disadvantaged inner-city youth. The ships usually sail in company and were built as 'twins' by the Los Angeles Maritime Institute in part to enable competition between the trainee crews.

National flag	USA
Home port	Los Angeles, California
Sparred length	33.7 m
Rig	Brigantine
Sail area	422 sq m
Gross tons	99
Hull material	Wood
Owner/operator	Los Angeles Maritime Institute
Built	Los Angeles, California
Launched	2002

W www.lamitopsail.org **E** director@lamitopsail.org

Photos: (right) Nancy Richardson

Opposite page: (top) Marann Fengler (bottom) Volker Corell

Eye of the Wind

Built in 1911, *Eye of the Wind* first served as a cargo ship for German and Swedish owners. She was rebuilt in 1973 by tall ship enthusiasts to become the flagship for Operation Drake, a two-year round-the-world scientific expedition under the patronage of HRH The Prince of Wales. She subsequently featured in Hollywood movies such as *Blue Lagoon*, *White Squall* and *Savage Island*. Today she operates throughout the year as a sail training ship for people of all ages, with a sailing programme that includes cruises, individual charters and on-board management training programmes in the seas around Europe, the North Atlantic, and Caribbean.

Photos: (below) Forum Train & Sail, (below right) Frank Anders

National flag	UK
Home port	St Helier, Jersey
Sparred length	40.23 m
Rig	Brig
Sail area	750 sq m
Gross tons	129
Hull material	Riveted steel
Owner/operator	FORUM Train & Sail, Germany
Built	Brake, Germany
Launched	1911

W www.eyeofthewind.net **E** info@eyeofthewind.net

Far Barcelona

Built in Norway in 1874 this ship, then called *Anne Dorthea*, was a fish transport vessel until 1975 when she was retired because the cost of her upkeep had become prohibitive. The Far Consortium in Barcelona acquired the vessel in 1996 and she was brought to the city to be restored. This work was undertaken over a period of many years by more than 300 young students (aged 16–25) and older unemployed people being trained in relevant trade skills. Since being restored, *Far Barcelona* has been used as a sail training ship for young people and for the development of environmental projects.

Photos: Pere de Prada

National flag	Spain
Home port	Barcelona
Sparred length	33 m
Rig	Schooner
Sail area	362 sq m
Gross tons	140
Hull material	Wood
Owner/operator	Consorci El Far
Built	Kvinnherad, Norway
Launched	1874 (relaunched 2006)

W www.consorcielfar.org
E informacio@consorcielfar.org

Fryderyk Chopin

Designed and built in 1992 as a sail training ship, *Fryderyk Chopin* is named after the famous Polish composer. Her debut voyage was to compete in the transatlantic Columbus Regatta for tall ships. Since then she has circumnavigated South America, undertaken annual voyages to the Caribbean and participated in the 2010 celebrations of International Chopin Year around Europe. Her owner runs conventional sail training programmes in European waters during the summer months and longer 'class afloat' voyages from Europe to the Caribbean during the autumn and winter semesters for high school students.

Photos: Jakub Pierzchała

National flag	Poland
Home port	Szczecin
Sparred length	55.5 m
Rig	Brig
Sail area	1,200 sq m
Gross tons	306
Hull material	Steel
Owner/operator	3Oceans
Built	Gdynia, Poland
Launched	1992

W www.fryderykchopin.pl **E** biuro@3oceans.pl

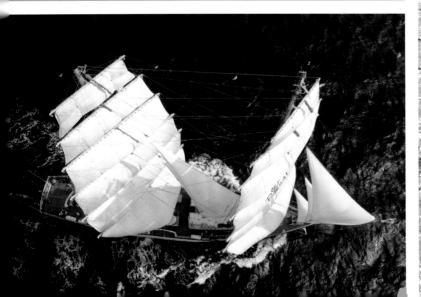

Georg Stage

The first *Georg Stage* was built in 1882 by the Danish ship owner Carl Frederik Stage as a training ship. Named after his deceased only son, she was donated to a foundation Carl Frederik had created to commemorate his son. The current *Georg Stage* was built in 1935 and continues to be operated as a sail training ship by the same foundation. The focus of her operation is young men and women aged 15–18. Most voyages take place between Sweden, Norway and the UK during the summer months. The ship is generally laid up during the winter months.

Photos: Stine Tanderup Pedersen

National flag	Denmark
Home port	Copenhagen
Sparred length	41 m
Rig	Full-rigged ship
Sail area	860 sq m
Gross tons	298
Hull material	Steel
Owner/operator	Georg Stage Stiftung
Built	Frederikshavn, Denmark
Launched	1935
W www.georgstage.dk	

HMS Gladan and HMS Falken

The Royal Swedish Navy has a very long tradition and commitment to sail training with sister ships. The *Gladan* (built first, defining a new design class) and *Falken* were built as twins in 1947 to replace two training ships that had been in service from the late 1800s. The *Gladan* and *Falken* sail mostly in the Baltic and North Sea, but occasionally also in the Mediterranean and transatlantic to the Caribbean and North America. While their principal role is to train officer cadets, they also provide training for the navy auxiliary corps and civilian students.

National flag	Sweden
Home port	Karlskrona
Sparred length	39.3 m
Rig	Schooner
Sail area	680 sq m
Gross tons	220
Hull material	Steel
Owner/operator	Royal Swedish Navy
Built	Stockholm, Sweden
Launched	1947

W blogg.forsvarsmakten.se/gladanochfalken
E falken.hms@gmail.com gladan.hms@gmail.com

Photos: Gladan and Falken Archive

Gloria

Colombia does not have a strong maritime heritage, but the commanding officer of the country's navy in the 1960s strongly believed in the value of sail training for navy cadets and persuaded the Minister of Defence to authorise the acquisition of a tall ship for this purpose. *Gloria* was built in Spain and launched in 1967. Named after the wife of the Minister of Defence, she is now the official flagship of the Colombian Navy. Like most navy-operated tall ships, she serves the dual purpose of sail training for cadets and roving international ambassador for her country.

Photos: (below) Max Mudie, (below right) Herbert H Boehm

National flag	Colombia
Home port	Cartagena, Colombia
Sparred length	76 m
Rig	Barque
Sail area	1,250 sq m
Displacement	1,330 tons
Hull material	Steel
Owner/operator	Colombian Navy
Built	Bilbao, Spain
Launched	1967
W www.armada.mil.co	

Gorch Fock

Built as a sail training ship for the Federal German Navy, *Gorch Fock* is named after a famous German author of sea stories who died at sea in the battle of Jutland during World War I. She has undergone a number of modifications since her launch in 1958 with major refurbishments in 1985, 2001, 2007 and 2011/12. Since coming into service she has trained some 15,000 cadets. *Gorch Fock* is a sister ship to USCG *Eagle* (USA), *Mircea* (Romania) and *Sagres* (Portugal).

Photos: German Navy

National flag	Germany
Home port	Kiel
Sparred length	89.32 m
Rig	Barque
Sail area	2,037 sq m
Displacement	1,760 tons
Hull material	Steel
Owner/operator	Federal German Navy
Built	Hamburg, Germany
Launched	1958
W www.gorchfock.de	

Götheborg

A replica of the 18th-century East Indiaman of the same name, the *Götheborg* is the world's largest operational wooden sailing vessel. The original *Götheborg* was owned by the Swedish East India Company and was returning from China in 1745 heavily laden with tea, porcelain and silver when she ran aground and sank just outside her home port of Gothenburg. Much of the cargo was saved, but it was not until the mid 1980s that what was left of the wreck was meticulously researched with a view to building a replica. The keel was laid in 1995, she was built using traditional methods in a purpose-built yard, and she was launched in 2003. Funding came from local business sponsorship and the general public. After lengthy sea trials her first voyage was to China. She is currently used for sail training and to promote cultural exchange, international relations and trade.

National flag	Sweden	
Home port	Gothenburg	
Sparred length	58.5 m	
Rig	Full-rigged ship	
Sail area	1,964 sq m	
Gross tons	788	
Hull material	Wood	
Owner/operator	Svenska Ostindiska Kompaniet AB	
Built	Gothenburg	
Launched	2003	
W www.soic.se **E** info@soic.se		

Photos: (right) Robin Aron Olsson

Opposite page: (top left) Brenda Wilson
(top right) Robin Aron Olsson
(bottom) Peder Jacobsson

Grossherzogin Elisabeth

Built at the beginning of the last century, this ship sailed worldwide as a freighter for 30 years. In the 1940s she was de-rigged and sailed under the Swedish flag as a coastal trader before being laid up. In 1973 she was rebuilt by a Hamburg ship owner to the original plans with a completely new rig. She was used for charter and passenger work in the Baltic, Mediterranean and Caribbean. From the early 1980s to 2006, renamed *Grossherzogin Elisabeth*, she served as a dormitory for cadets at the merchant marine school in Elsfleth, Germany. Since then she has been used as a training ship and for charter work in the North Sea and the Baltic.

Photos: Axel Wolkowski

National flag	Germany
Home port	Elsfleth
Sparred length	66 m
Rig	Gaff schooner
Sail area	1,010 sq m
Gross tons	489
Hull material	Steel
Owner/operator	Schulschiffverein Grossherzogin Elisabeth
Built	Alblasserdam, Netherlands
Launched	1909
W www.grossherzogin-elisabeth.de	

Guayas

Guayas is operated by the Ecuador Navy as a sail training ship for navy cadets and as an ambassador for the country. She is the sister ship of the Colombian Navy's *Gloria*, built ten years earlier by the same yard in Spain. Guayas was a tribal chief in Ecuador. It is also the name of the country's largest river.

Photos: Herbert H Boehm

National flag	Ecuador
Home port	Guayaquil
Sparred length	78.40 m
Rig	Barque
Sail area	1,410 sq m
Displacement	1,300 tons
Hull material	Steel
Owner/operator	Ecuador Navy
Built	Bilbao, Spain
Launched	1976
W www.besgua.armada.mil.ec	

Gulden Leeuw

Gulden Leeuw (Golden Lion) was built in 1937 by the Danish government as an ocean-going ice-class ship and was later used as both an offshore support vessel and a training ship for the Danish Nautical School. She was bought in 2007 by her current owners and converted to a three-masted topsail schooner. She is used for sail training and passenger cruising, mainly in the North Sea and Baltic and occasionally further afield. She is owned by two Dutch couples who have known each other since childhood: Arjen and Charissa Töller and Robert and Mirjam Postuma. Arjen and Robert alternate as the vessel's captain.

Photos: Richard Sibley

National flag	Netherlands
Home port	Kampen
Sparred length	70.10 m
Rig	Topsail schooner
Sail area	1,545 sq m
Gross tons	487
Hull material	Steel
Owner/operator	Töller and Postuma families
Built	Frederikshavn, Denmark
Launched	1937 (relaunched 2010)

W www.guldenleeuw.com **E** info@guldenleeuw.com

Gunilla

Although *Gunilla* was built in 1940, she did not come into service until 1945 at the end of World War II. She was rigged as a schooner and used as a short-haul freighter. In 1954 she was lengthened by eight metres and converted to a pure motor ship. She was later acquired by an organisation called Sailing

Schools for Better Knowledge and converted to a barque. Today, *Gunilla* is owned and operated by the AB Gunilla shipping company as a sail training ship for a wide range of students. Training voyages take place in Swedish waters, and occasionally to the Caribbean and South America.

Photos: Jörgen Hansson

National flag	Sweden
Home port	Öckerö
Sparred length	61 m
Rig	Barque
Sail area	1,040 sq m
Gross tons	402
Hull material	Steel
Owner/operator	AB Gunilla
Built	Oskarshamn, Sweden
Launched	1940

W www.gunilla.nu **E** gunilla@gunilla.nu

Harvey Gamage, Spirit of Massachusetts and Westward

All three ships are owned and operated by the Ocean Classroom Foundation and offer similar educational programmes. Voyages range from one week to four months in duration, with destinations in Canada, the US East Coast and the Caribbean. Secondary school and university students are taught academic subjects as well as traditional seamanship, and academic credits are earned on the longer programmes. *Harvey Gamage*

is typical of freight-carrying vessels operating in US coastal waters in the mid to late 1800s. The design of *Spirit of Massachusetts* was inspired by the Fredonia class of Gloucester fishing schooners that operated in the North Atlantic in the late 1800s. *Westward* was built as a private yacht, then served as the flagship for Sea Education Afloat before being acquired by the Ocean Classroom Foundation in 2004.

Harvey Gamage (HG), Spirit of Massachusetts (SoM), Westward (W)	
National flag	USA
Home port	Islesboro, Maine (HG), Boston, Mass (SoM), Rockland, Maine (W)
Sparred length	40.03 m (HG), 38.5 m (SoM), 38.5 m (W)
Rig	Gaff topsail schooner (HG and SoM), staysail schooner (W)
Sail area	473 sq m (HG), 663 sq m (SoM), 615 sq m (W)
Gross tons	94 (HG), 90 (SoM), 114 (W)
Hull material	Wood (HG and SoM), steel (W)
Owner/operator	Ocean Classroom Foundation
Built	Bristol, Maine (HG), Boston, Mass (SoM), Lemwerder, Germany (W)
Launched	1973 (HG), 1984 (SoM), 1961 (W)
W www.oceanclassroom.org **E** mail@oceanclassroom.org	

Photos: Ocean Classroom Foundation

Helena

Helena was built in Finland as a gaff schooner in 1991–1992 and launched in the spring of 1992. Her primary use is sail training. She covered a staggering 560,000 nautical miles during her first 20 years of operation (the equivalent of a complete circumnavigation every year) before a major refit in 2012 when she was also re-rigged as a Bermudan schooner. She has rounded Cape Horn, visited Tristan da Cunha, crossed the 80th parallel at Svalbard and crossed the Atlantic 38 times. *Helena* sails a punishing average of 330 days per year.

National flag	Finland
Home port	Turku
Sparred length	39.5 m
Rig	Bermudan schooner
Sail area	550 sq m
Gross tons	110
Hull material	Wood (oak)
Owner/operator	Sail Training Association Finland
Built	Uusikaupunki, Finland
Launched	1992 (total refit 2012)

W www.staf.fi **E** helena@staf.fi

Photos: (right) Atte Joutsen

Opposite page: (top) Tuomo Pöntinen (bottom) Tim Wright

ORP Iskra

Designed by Polish naval architect Zygmunt Choreń, *Iskra* has a different rig on each of her three masts. She is a sister ship to *Pogoria* (Poland) and *Kaliakra* (Bulgaria), which were also built in Gdansk. Since 1982 *Iskra* has sailed more than 200,000 nautical miles and visited 30 countries around the world, mainly with cadets of the Polish Navy. During the summer months she also sails with young trainees from schools and youth organisations. Her predecessor, also called *Iskra*, sailed 250,000 nautical miles and trained more than 4,000 cadets in her 50 years of service (1927–1977).

National flag	Poland
Home port	Gdynia
Sparred length	49 m
Rig	Barquentine
Sail area	1,035 sq m
Displacement	381 tons
Hull material	Steel
Owner/operator	Polish Navy
Built	Gdansk, Poland
Launched	1982

W www.facebook.com/iskraORP **E** iskra@poczta.fm

Photos: Bartek Ciesielski

Italia

Nave Italia claims to be the largest sailing brigantine in the world. Owned by the Italian Navy, she is a training vessel for Italian Navy cadets and other young people but also serves a number of other purposes. She can accommodate 30 guests in luxurious accommodation and is used for a range of research and education as well as social and ambassadorial projects.

Photos: Cinefoto – Marina Militare Italiana

National flag	Italy
Home port	Genova
Sparred length	61 m
Rig	Brigantine
Sail area	1,300 sq m
Gross tons	480
Hull material	Steel
Owner/operator	Italian Navy
Built	Gdansk, Poland
Launched	1993

W www.naveitalia.org **E** info@naveitalia.org

Jadran

Jadran is a sailing school ship built for the Yugoslav Navy. Her name means 'Adriatic' and most of the ship's training voyages are undertaken in the Mediterranean. She was commandeered during World War II by Italy and sailed as *Marco Polo*. She was then used as a floating bridge in one of the canals in Venice. After the war she was returned to Yugoslavia where she underwent major refurbishment. Further reconstruction was undertaken in the mid 1950s and again in the 1960s when she was almost completely rebuilt. Today she is operated by the Navy of Montenegro.

Photos: Montenegro Navy

National flag	Montenegro
Home port	Tivat
Sparred length	60 m
Rig	Barquentine
Sail area	933 sq m
Displacement	787 tons
Hull material	Steel
Owner/operator	Montenegro Navy
Built	Hamburg, Germany
Launched	1931

W www.vojska.me **E** goran.pajovic@vojska.me

James Craig

First launched in 1874 as *Clan Macleod*, this ship was acquired by a New Zealand businessman, JJ Craig, in 1900 and served as a cargo ship until 1925. She was then used as a coal hulk in Recherche Bay, Tasmania, and abandoned in 1932 when she broke her moorings and became beached during a storm. She was acquired by the Sydney Heritage Fleet in 1972 and began a meticulous A$30 million restoration that took nearly 40 years of volunteer effort. She was relaunched in 1997 and began operations in 2001. She is now used for day-sailing and longer charter work and occasionally as a sail training ship.

Photos: (below) Mark McNicol, (below right) Calvin Gardiner

National flag	Australia
Home port	Sydney
Sparred length	70 m
Rig	Barque
Sail area	1,100 sq m
Gross tons	671
Hull material	Wrought iron and steel
Owner/operator	Sydney Maritime Museum (Sydney Heritage Fleet)
Built	Sunderland, UK (rebuilt Sydney)
Launched	1874 (relaunched 1997)
W www.shf.org.au **E** info@shf.org.au	

Jens Krogh

Jens Krogh was built in 1899 for fishing in the North Sea. In 1973 FDF Aalborg Søkreds, a youth organisation, rebuilt her as a sail training vessel and brought her back to her original ketch rig. Managed and sailed entirely by volunteers, *Jens Krogh* operates routinely in most of the seas around Europe. Since 1980 she has taken part in nearly every event organised by Sail Training International, including the annual Tall Ships Races series in Europe, two Atlantic crossings and the Hong Kong–Osaka Tall Ships Race.

Photos: (below) Snorre Aske, (below right) Morten Frederiksen

National flag	Denmark
Home port	Aalborg
Sparred length	24.5 m
Rig	Ketch
Sail area	230 sq m
Gross tons	34.45
Hull material	Wood (oak)
Owner/operator	FDF Aalborg Søkreds
Built	Frederikshavn, Denmark
Launched	1899

W: www.jenskrogh.dk **E**: jenskrogh@jenskrogh.dk

Johann Smidt

Built in 1974 as a sail training ship for young people, the vessel was acquired by her current owners in 1989 and renamed *Johann Smidt* after a former mayor of Bremen. Her purpose has remained the same, sail training for young people. During the summer months she operates conventional sail training programmes of 7–14 days' duration, mostly in the Baltic Sea. From October to May she sails from Hamburg to the Caribbean as a sailing classroom for secondary school students from a local school under a programme called 'High Seas High School'.

Photos: Simona Dittrich-Knüppel

National flag	Germany
Home port	Bremen
Sparred length	35.95 m
Rig	Gaff schooner
Sail area	471 sq m
Gross tons	146
Hull material	Steel
Owner/operator	Clipper DJS
Built	Amsterdam, Netherlands
Launched	1974

W www.clipper-djs.org **E** buero@clipper-djs.org

Jolie Brise

This famous vessel, built in France just over a century ago, has been operated by Dauntsey's School in England since 1977 as an important element of the school's experiential learning programme. Prior to that she was owned for 30 years by Dr Luis Lobato, founder of the Portuguese Sail Training Association. Since 1977 the vessel has been maintained by the pupils of Dauntsey's and some 6,500 pupils have sailed in her, covering more than 175,000 nautical miles, mostly in the waters around the UK but also further afield in Europe and occasionally across the Atlantic.

Photos: Rick Tomlinson

National flag	UK
Home port	Hamble
Sparred length	25 m
Rig	Gaff cutter
Sail area	311 sq m
Gross tons	44
Hull material	Wood (oak)
Owner/operator	Dauntsey's School
Built	Le Havre, France
Launched	1913

W www.joliebrise.com **E** marristr@dauntseys.wilts.sch.uk

Juan Sebastián de Elcano

Built in 1928, *Juan Sebastián de Elcano* continues to serve as the midshipman training ship for the Spanish Navy and as a 'floating embassy' supporting Spanish foreign policy. In this capacity, she has sailed around the world ten times and visited more than 180 ports in 70 countries. She is named after a famous Spanish sailor who was a member of the expedition team headed by Magellan in the early 1500s to find a western route to the Spice Islands. Three years after the expedition left, only a handful of men returned to Spain, led by Elcano, the first in history to circumnavigate.

National flag	Spain
Home port	San Fernando
Sparred length	113 m
Rig	Topsail schooner
Sail area	3,151 sq m
Displacement	3,771 tons
Hull material	Steel
Owner/operator	Spanish Navy
Built	Cádiz, Spain
Launched	1928

W www.armada.mde.es
E elcano.armada@amosconnect.com

Photos: Armada Española

Kaliakra

Built in 1984 as a sail training ship for the Navigation Maritime Bulgare (Bulgarian national shipping company) to help train merchant marine and navy cadets, *Kaliakra* also served as an international ambassador for the country. In 2008, ownership of *Kaliakra* was transferred to the Bulgarian Maritime Training Centre. Her principal purpose remains training young people for a career at sea, but she is also used for other youth sail training programmes and charter work.

Photos: Kaliakra Archive

National flag	Bulgaria
Home port	Varna
Sparred length	52 m
Rig	Barquentine
Sail area	1,080 sq m
Gross tons	247
Hull material	Steel
Owner/operator	Bulgarian Maritime Training Centre
Built	Gdansk, Poland
Launched	1984

W kaliakra.bmtc-bg.com **E** kaliakra@bmtc.bg

Khersones

The ship was designed and built for sail training, but today she is also used for charter and passenger voyages. She is one of the few sailing ships to have circumnavigated South America in an anti-clockwise direction from 50°S in the Pacific to 50°S in the Atlantic. The ship is named after the ancient city of Chersonesos on the Crimean peninsula (now the site of Sevastopol).

Photos: Kerch State University

National flag	Ukraine
Home port	Kerch
Sparred length	109.40 m
Rig	Full-rigged ship
Sail area	2,771 sq m
Gross tons	2,264
Hull material	Steel
Owner/operator	Naval Technology Institute, Kerch
Built	Gdansk, Poland
Launched	1989
W www.khersones-x.de	

Kruzenshtern

Built in 1928 for the German shipping company F Laeisz as a combined freighter and school ship (then called *Padua*), *Kruzenshtern* traded initially between Europe and South America (saltpetre) and then between Europe and Australia (wheat). Ownership was transferred to Russia in 1946 as war reparations and the ship was renamed after Adam Johann Ritter von Krusenstern, a famous 18th-century Russian seaman and explorer. She circumnavigated in the mid 1990s and again in 2005–2006 to celebrate the 200th anniversary of Adam von Krusenstern's circumnavigation. She is operated today by the Baltic Fishing Fleet State Academy as a sail training ship, but also sails with passengers through the German organisation 'Friends of the *Kruzenshtern*'.

National flag	Russia
Home port	Kaliningrad
Sparred length	114.50 m
Rig	Barque
Sail area	3,400 sq m
Displacement	5,805 tons
Hull material	Steel
Owner/operator	Baltic Fishing Fleet State Academy
Built	Bremerhaven, Germany
Launched	1926

W www.kruzenshtern.info **E** mail@bffsa.com

Photos: Vasiliy Semidyanov

Lady Nelson

The original *Lady Nelson* was built in England in 1798 and sent by the Royal Navy to Australia (then called New Holland) as a survey and exploration vessel. While collecting livestock in the Indonesian archipelago in 1825 for settlement in northern Australia the ship was attacked and burned and all the crew murdered. Built in Tasmania, the current *Lady Nelson* is an almost exact replica of the original ship. In addition to serving as a sail training vessel, she is used for day-sailing in Hobart harbour and for both inshore and offshore charter work.

Photos: (below) Lady Nelson Archive, (below right) Julie Porter

National flag	Australia
Home port	Hobart
Sparred length	25.76 m
Rig	Brig
Sail area	215.9 sq m
Gross tons	70
Hull material	Wood (Tasmanian blue gum and celery-top pine)
Owner/operator	Tasmanian Sail Training Association
Built	Woodbridge, Tasmania
Launched	1988

W www.ladynelson.org.au **E** enquiries@ladynelson.org.au

Lady Washington

The brig *Lady Washington* is a replica of one of the first US-flagged ships to visit the west coast of North America. In the late 1780s, the original *Lady Washington* sailed from Boston around Cape Horn to trade for sea otter pelts with the native tribes on what would later be called Vancouver Island. She also sailed to Japan, Hawaii and Hong Kong. Launched in 1989 at Aberdeen, Washington, to celebrate Washington State's centennial, the modern *Lady Washington* visits more than 40 ports a year on the west coast of the USA and Canada and conducts living history education programmes for elementary and secondary schools and the general public. She has appeared in several films including the 2003 *Pirates of the Caribbean: the Curse of the Black Pearl*.

Photos: (below) Tom Hyde, (below right) Ron Arel

National flag	USA
Home port	Aberdeen, Washington
Sparred length	34.1 m
Rig	Brig
Sail area	1,354 sq m
Gross tons	99
Hull material	Wood
Owner/operator	Grays Harbor Historical Seaport Authority
Built	Aberdeen, Washington
Launched	1989
W www.historicalseaport.org	
E admin@historicalseaport.org	

Leeuwin II

The largest of Australia's sail training tall ships, *Leeuwin II* was built specifically to 'inspire and challenge the youth of Western Australia to reach their full potential' and to recognise Western Australia's strong maritime heritage. The original *Leeuwin*, a Dutch ship, rounded the continent's south-western cape (subsequently named Cape Leeuwin) in 1622. The Leeuwin Ocean Adventure Foundation's sail training programmes range from three-hour taster sails, including ones for primary school children, to more conventional seven-day youth explorer voyages and shorter specialist programmes for young people with physical or learning disabilities. Funding from government, youth charities and commercial organisations and a large pool of volunteer crew are key to the foundation's survival.

National flag	Australia
Home port	Fremantle
Sparred length	55 m
Rig	Barquentine
Sail area	810 sq m
Displacement	344 tons
Hull material	Welded steel
Owner/operator	Leeuwin Ocean Adventure Foundation
Built	Henderson, Australia
Launched	1986

W www.sailleeuwin.com **E** office@sailleeuwin.com

Photos: Ocean Adventure Foundation

ARA Libertad

The ninth Argentine Navy vessel to bear this name, *Libertad* ('Freedom') was first conceived in 1946 and launched in 1956, but only came into service as the country's naval sail training tall ship in 1963. Since then she has sailed more than 900,000 nautical miles, visited some 520 ports in 62 countries and trained more than 10,000 officers, navy cadets and sailors. She has also participated in a wide range of maritime festivals and events around the world. *Libertad* was designated by presidential decree as an 'Honorary Embassy of the Republic' in 2001. The Argentine Navy has operated a tall ship to help train navy cadets at sea since 1873.

Photos: Silvina Rossello

National flag	Argentina
Home port	Buenos Aires
Sparred length	103.75 m
Rig	Full-rigged ship
Sail area	2,643 sq m
Displacement	3,765 metric tonnes
Hull material	Steel
Owner/operator	Argentine Navy
Built	Astillero Río Santiago, Argentina
Launched	1956

W www.ara.mil.ar **E** webmaster@ara.mil.ar

Liv

Not a conventional 'tall ship' in the accepted understanding of the term, *Liv* is a very interesting sail training vessel because of her extraordinary history. She was built in 1893 as a rescue vessel in the north of Norway. In nearly 40 years of service she assisted 1,338 vessels in trouble and saved 132 lives. In 1932 ownership was transferred to the police service and *Liv* became a fisheries patrol vessel. From 1942 to 1963 she was used as a ferry, certified to carry 60 people, a remarkable number given her size. She was then bought by a Norwegian couple, Inger and Terje Smith, who sold their house to finance her restoration and then sailed her around the world. She is still owned by the family and used for sail training.

Photos: (below) Alexander Borg, (below right) Knut K Gransæter

National flag	Norway
Home port	Blommenholm (Oslo)
Sparred length	17 m
Rig	Gaff ketch
Sail area	127 sq m
Gross tons	22.8
Hull material	Wood (oak)
Owner/operator	Inger and Terje Smith
Built	Porsgrunn, Norway
Launched	1893
E te-smi@online.no	

Lord Nelson and Tenacious

These are the only two tall ships in the world designed and operated to enable people of all physical abilities to sail together as equals. The design of the ships enables people in wheelchairs to move freely both on deck and below. On-board technical equipment (e.g. speaking compass and hearing loop) enables the blind and deaf to navigate and steer the ships unaided.

The Jubilee Sailing Trust charity was founded in 1978 with start-up funding from the Queen's Silver Jubilee Appeal Fund. Additional funds were raised to enable the building of *Lord Nelson* in 1985. *Tenacious* was built 15 years later. Bringing ashore the trust's charitable aims of integrating people of all abilities, *Tenacious* was built by a mixed-ability team.

Lord Nelson (LN), Tenacious (T)

National flag	UK
Home port	Southampton
Sparred length	54.7 m (LN), 65 m (T)
Rig	Barque
Sail area	1,024 sq m (LN), 1,200 sq m (T)
Gross tons	368 (LN), 586 (T)
Hull material	Steel (LN), wood/epoxy laminate (T)
Owner/operator	Jubilee Sailing Trust
Built	Wivenhoe, UK (LN), Southampton, UK (T)
Launched	1985 (LN), 2000 (T)

W www.jst.org.uk **E** info@jst.org.uk

Photos: (right) Max Mudie

Opposite page: (top left) Sail Training International (top right and bottom) Max Mudie

Mir

Sharing her name with Russia's space station (1986–2001), *Mir* was designed and built as a sail training ship in 1987. Mir means 'world' and 'peace', reflecting her mission. She acts as St Petersburg's 'Envoy of Friendship', particularly during foreign voyages. Most of the year she sails with cadets from the Admiral Makarov State University of Maritime and Inland Shipping in St Petersburg and maritime institutions from elsewhere in Russia and other countries. She also undertakes charter work and day-sailing for tourists.

National flag	Russia
Home port	St Petersburg
Sparred length	110 m
Rig	Full-rigged ship
Sail area	2,771 sq m
Gross tons	2257
Hull material	Steel
Owner/operator	Admiral Makarov State University of Maritime and Inland Shipping
Built	Gdansk, Poland
Launched	1987

W www.tall-shipmir.ru **E** mir@gma.ru

Photos: (right) Mir Archive

Opposite page: (top left) John Cadd (top right and bottom) Mir Archive

Mircea

Mircea was built in Germany just before World War II as a sail training ship for the Romanian Navy. She is named after the 14th-century Duke of Mircea. She underwent a major refit and refurbishment in 1966 and again in 2002. During her 70+ years of service she has sailed more than 400,000 nautical miles and provided training for about 50,000 cadets from Romania and a number of other countries.

Photos: Mircea cel Batran Naval Academy

National flag	Romania
Home port	Constanta
Sparred length	82.10 m
Rig	Barque
Sail area	1,748 sq m
Gross tons	1,312
Hull material	Steel
Owner/operator	Maritime School Constanta
Built	Hamburg, Germany
Launched	1938

W www.anmb.ro **E** relatiipublice@anmb.ro

Morgenster

Built in 1919 as a North Sea fishing lugger, *Morgenster* underwent a major restoration and rebuild in 2006 in Alphen/Urk when her rig was changed to a clipper brig. A central mission of the ship's owner is to preserve maritime heritage and practices. The ship undertakes sail training voyages, day-sails and passage-making trips for tourists.

Photos: (below) Morgenster Archive, (below right) Herbert H Boehm

National flag	Netherlands
Home port	Den Helder
Sparred length	48 m
Rig	Brig
Sail area	650 sq m
Gross tons	159
Hull material	Steel
Owner/operator	Harry Muter
Built	Alphen, Netherlands
Launched	1919

W www.zeilbrik.org **E** info@zeilbrik.org

Nadezhda

This ship was built for the Russian Maritime State University in Vladivostok to serve a number of purposes. Key among them was to provide sail training programmes for cadets at the university, participation in the annual Far Eastern Floating University programme, marine research with the Russian Academy of Science, and promoting awareness of maritime history and environmental issues among the general public. *Nadezhda* has undertaken many extended voyages in the Asia/Pacific region and circumnavigated in 2003–2004. In 2011 she participated in the international monitoring of the marine environmental impact of the Fukushima nuclear power station disaster in Japan.

Photos: (below) Alexsandr Seleznev, (below right) Vitaliy Nikolaev

National flag	Russia
Home port	Vladivostok
Sparred length	108.6 m
Rig	Full-rigged ship
Sail area	2,768 sq m
Displacement	2,800 tons
Hull material	Steel
Owner/operator	Admiral G I Nevelskoy Maritime State University
Built	Gdansk, Poland
Launched	1992

W www.msun.ru **E** sts_nadezhda@morsatmail.com

Niagara

The original *Niagara*, of which this ship is a replica, served as the relief flagship of Commodore Oliver Hazard Perry whose small fleet defeated the British in the Battle of Lake Erie during the War of 1812. The ship sank in 1820 but was raised almost 100 years later and underwent a major restoration. However, she was scrapped in 1988 and parts of the ship were preserved and worked into the replica launched in the same year. *Niagara* is registered as a sailing school ship. She operates a three-week training programme for people of all ages throughout the year and is a tourist attraction in her home port of Erie, Pennsylvania.

Photos: (below) Robert Lowry, (below right) John Baker

National flag	USA
Home port	Erie, Pennsylvania
Sparred length	60.35 m
Rig	Brig
Sail area	1,077.6 sq m
Gross tons	162
Hull material	Wood
Owner/operator	Commonwealth of Pennsylvania/ Flagship Niagara League
Built	Erie, Pennsylvania
Launched	1988
W	www.flagshipniagara.org
E	marineops@flagshipniagara.org

Nippon Maru and Kaiwo Maru

These ships are almost identical, built five years apart at the same yard. They both have government support but are operated by different independent administrative institutions. *Nippon Maru* replaced a ship of the same name and between them they have provided comprehensive training for merchant marine cadets for more than half a century. *Kaiwo Maru* also replaced a ship of the same name. Her predecessor was used exclusively as a training ship for merchant marine cadets. However, the current *Kaiwo Maru* was built to serve as a floating classroom and platform for experimental voyaging for a wider cross-section of young people, as well as for training merchant marine cadets.

Nippon Maru (NM), Kaiwo Maru (KM)

National flag	Japan
Home port	Tokyo
Sparred length	110.9 m
Rig	Barque
Sail area	2,760 sq m
Gross tons	2,891 (NM), 2,879 (KM)
Hull material	Steel
Owner/operator	National Institute for Sea Training (NM), Training Ship Education Support Association (KM)
Built	Uraga, Japan
Launched	1984 (NM), 1989 (KM)

W www.kohkun.go.jp E mail@kohkun.go.jp

Photos: Tsuneo Nakamura

Oosterschelde

Built as a freighter for transatlantic trade in 1917, *Oosterschelde* underwent a very careful restoration between 1988 and 1992. Two years' research into the ship's historical records were followed by a restoration programme supervised by maritime museums to ensure authenticity in the detail of both design and materials. The ship is registered as a monument by the Dutch Ministry of Culture. Since her restoration, she has sailed around the world and visited 45 countries on five continents. In addition to conducting sail training voyages and expeditions, the ship is frequently used for charter work (day-sailing and longer voyages) and in-port corporate hospitality events.

National flag	Netherlands
Home port	Rotterdam
Sparred length	50 m
Rig	Topsail schooner
Sail area	890 sq m
Gross tons	226
Hull material	Riveted steel
Owner/operator	Shipping Company Oosterschelde
Built	Zwartsluis, Netherlands
Launched	1918

W www.oosterschelde.nl E info@oosterschelde.nl

Photos: (right) Oosterschelde Archive

Opposite page: (top left) Arthur Smeets
(top right) Kai Dieho
(bottom) Pieter Nijdeken

Pacific Swift and Pacific Grace

Both ships were built for the Sail and Life Training Society (SALTS) and both generally operate a programme of five- to ten-day sail training voyages for young people (as well as day-sails for SALTS members) along the coast of British Columbia. But both have also undertaken more exotic voyages. Launched in 1986, *Pacific Swift* has sailed to Australia and Europe, to remote communities in Easter and Pitcairn Islands and to many other unusual and far-flung ports of call. Launched in 1999, *Pacific Grace* embarked on her maiden offshore voyage to the South Pacific in 2003. In 2007–2008 she undertook another major voyage to ports in 15 countries in the Pacific, including China and Japan. On both expeditions she was crewed by young people aged 17–25.

Pacific Swift (PS), Pacific Grace (PG)

National flag	Canada
Home port	Victoria, BC
Sparred length	34 m (PS), 42 m (PG)
Rig	Topsail schooner (PS), gaff schooner (PG)
Sail area	510 sq m (PS), 740 sq m (PG)
Gross tons	71.45 (PS), 94 (PG)
Hull material	Wood
Owner/operator	Sail and Life Training Society (SALTS)
Built	Vancouver, Canada (PS), Victoria, Canada (PG)
Launched	1986 (PS), 1999 (PG)

W: www.salts.ca **E**: info@salts.ca

Photos: (right) Sam Vaale

Opposite page: (top left) Mark Kaarremaa
(top right) Larochelle Images
(bottom) Emmy Phillips.

Palinuro

Built in 1934 as a barquentine and sailed under the French flag, *Palinuro* was acquired by the Italian Navy in 1951 and converted to a schooner for use as a sail training ship for navy cadets from the military school in Taranto. Named *Palinuro* after Aeneas's navigator in Graeco-Roman mythology, she was originally mainly used to train helmsmen. She underwent a second major overhaul and refit in 1984–1986.

Photos: Cinefoto–Marina Militare Italiana

National flag	Italy
Home port	La Spezia
Sparred length	69 m
Rig	Schooner
Sail area	1,000 sq m
Gross tons	1,341
Hull material	Wood and steel
Owner/operator	Italian Navy
Built	Nantes, France
Launched	1934

W www.marina.difesa.it/uominimezzi/navi/Pagine/Palinuro.aspx **E** palinuro@marina.difesa.

Pelican of London

Built in 1948 as a deep-water trawler and named *Le Pelican*, this barquentine has a hull design based on the French clippers of the 1870s. She subsequently traded in the Baltic but in 1993 was caught trafficking a cargo of contraband vodka from Finland and confiscated by customs. The vessel was acquired from the customs authorities by a British entrepreneur and sailing enthusiast who saw her potential for conversion to a sail training tall ship. This was accomplished in 2007 by a partnership he had established for the purpose. The ship was renamed *Pelican of London* and a charity, Adventure Under Sail, was created by the partnership in 2008 to operate her as a sail training vessel with a particular focus on the development of young people. She is also used for charter work.

Photos: Connor Sexton

National flag	UK
Home port	Weymouth
Sparred length	45 m
Rig	Barquentine
Sail area	525 sq m
Gross tons	226
Hull material	Steel
Owner/operator	Adventure Under Sail
Built	Le Havre, France
Launched	1948 (relaunched 2007)

W www.adventureundersail.com
E enquiries@adventureundersail.com

Picton Castle

Picton Castle was built in 1928 as a fishing trawler. In World War II she was pressed into service with the British Royal Navy as a minesweeper and convoy escort. Following the war, she returned to fishing and subsequently carried cargo around the North Sea. In the 1990s, as Captain Daniel Moreland was looking for a vessel with classic sailing ship hull lines, he found her lying in Norway. He purchased her and brought her to Lunenburg, Nova Scotia, in Canada, where she was refitted as a three-masted barque for sail training. Since her refit, *Picton Castle* has circumnavigated five times and sailed to Europe, Africa, the Caribbean, the Great Lakes and the east coast of North America on numerous voyages.

National flag	Cook Islands
Home port	Avatiu, Rarotonga, Cook Islands
Sparred length	54 m
Rig	Barque
Sail area	1,160 sq m
Gross tons	284
Hull material	Riveted steel
Owner/operator	Windward Isles Sailing Ship Company
Built	Selby, England
Launched	1928 (rebuilt 1955, refit 1996–97)

W: www.picton-castle.com **E**: info@picton-castle.com

Photos: Picton Castle Archive

Pogoria

Built as a sailing school ship for the Iron Shackle Association of Poland in 1980, *Pogoria* is now owned and operated by the Sail Training Association Poland. In the early 1980s, she sailed to Antarctica on a commission from the Polish Academy of Sciences. In the late 1980s and early 1990s she was chartered by the Canadian Educational Alternative as a floating classroom. Under the ownership of the Sail Training Association Poland she provides sail training for young people throughout the summer months and at other times of year undertakes charter voyages, often to the Caribbean.

National flag	Poland
Home port	Gdynia
Sparred length	47 m
Rig	Barquentine
Sail area	1,000 sq m
Gross tons	291
Hull material	Steel
Owner/operator	Sail Training Association Poland
Built	Gdansk, Poland
Launched	1980

W www.pogoria.pl **E** pogoria@pogoria.pl

Photos: Sail Training Association Poland

Pride of Baltimore II

The design of the *Pride of Baltimore II* is based on the classic 19th-century Maryland privateers. She was built for Pride of Baltimore Inc., a non-profit organisation dedicated to preserving and promoting the maritime history of the Chesapeake Bay area through education and traditional nautical skills. She is used as a sail training vessel and also serves as a platform for scientific, environmental and social studies. The original Maryland privateers, of which there were about 200, were well armed and ran a blockade against the British in the War of 1812. The most famous of them was the *Chasseur* which, in a daring raid across the Atlantic, captured 17 British ships and thus earned the nickname 'Pride of Baltimore'.

Photos: Greg Pease

National flag	USA
Home port	Baltimore, Maryland
Sparred length	47.85 m
Rig	Schooner
Sail area	837.8 sq m
Gross tons	115
Hull material	Wood
Owner/operator	Pride of Baltimore Inc.
Built	Baltimore, Maryland
Launched	1988

W: www.pride2.org **E**: pride2@pride2.org

R Tucker Thompson

Work on the *R Tucker Thompson* began in the 1970s by Robert Tucker Thompson and his son Tod, but she was not finished until the mid 1980s. Robert died while she was under construction and the vessel was later completed by Tod and business partner Russell Harris. The design of the *R Tucker Thompson* is based on the halibut schooners that plied their trade on the US West Coast in the early 19th century. She is now owned by a charitable trust established to run youth development voyages during the New Zealand winter months. The trust runs cruises for tourists in the Bay of Islands during summer months to help fund the youth programmes and maintenance.

Photos: R Tucker Thompson Archive

National flag	New Zealand
Home port	Opua
Sparred length	25.9 m
Rig	Topsail schooner
Sail area	278.7 sq m
Gross tons	44
Hull material	Steel
Owner/operator	R Tucker Thompson Sail Training Trust
Built	Mangawhai, New Zealand
Launched	1985

W www.tucker.co.nz E info@tucker.co.nz

PNS Rah Naward

PNS *Rah Naward* was built as a sail training ship for the UK's Sail Training Association and named *Prince William* (a sister ship to the *Stavros S Niarchos* built at the same time for the same organisation). Both hulls had been built in Germany in 1996, but their completion as brigantines for use as luxury cruisers in the Caribbean was abandoned. They were acquired by the Sail Training Association in 1997 and completed as brigs in 2000. The *Prince William* was sold in 2011 to the Pakistan Navy and is used as a sailing school ship. PNS *Rah Naward* is the Pakistan Navy's first ever sail training tall ship.

Photos: Pakistan Navy

National flag	Pakistan
Home port	Karachi
Sparred length	59.35 m
Rig	Brig
Sail area	949 sq m
Gross tons	493
Hull material	Steel
Owner/operator	Pakistan Navy
Built	Lemwerder, Germany and Appledore, UK
Launched	2000
W	www.paknavy.gov.pk

Roald Amundsen

Designed and built to be a deep-sea fishing lugger in the early 1950s, *Roald Amundsen* was owned by the East German Army for a short while before being acquired by the not-for-profit organisation Leben Lernen auf Segelschiffen (Learning to live on board sailing ships), which converted her to a sail training ship. Her first voyage in this capacity was in 1993. Since then she has sailed with trainees and an all-volunteer crew throughout the year, mainly in the Baltic, North Sea and North Atlantic during summer months and the Mediterranean and Canary Islands (with occasional transatlantic voyages) during the winter.

Photos: Roald Amundsen Archive

National flag	Germany
Home port	Eckernförde
Sparred length	50.2 m
Rig	Brig
Sail area	850 sq m
Gross tons	298
Hull material	Riveted steel
Owner/operator	Leben Lernen auf Segelschiffen
Built	Rosslau, Germany
Launched	1952 (relaunched 1993)

W www.sailtraining.de **E** office@sailtraining.de

TS Royalist

The smallest square-rigged sail training ship in operation, *Royalist* was built for the Sea Cadets, a UK charity based on the customs and traditions of the Royal Navy. She provides sail training opportunities to young people aged 13½–18. She operates throughout the year with voyages of up to a week in UK and near Continental waters. Since commissioning, more than 30,000 sea cadets have sailed on her. A new ship is being built in Spain to replace *Royalist* in 2015.

Photos: (below) Sail Training International, (below right) Marine Society & Sea Cadets

National flag	UK
Home port	Portsmouth
Sparred length	29.12 m
Rig	Brig
Sail area	452 sq m
Gross tons	83
Hull material	Steel
Owner/operator	Marine Society & Sea Cadets (MSSC)
Built	Cowes, UK
Launched	1971

W www.sea-cadets.org **E** offshoreoffice@ms-sc.org

Rupel

The Belgian training ship *Rupel* was built over a five-year period in the 1990s by long-term unemployed people as a social project for communities bordering the River Rupel, upstream from Antwerp. Since her launch in 1996 she has sailed some 75,000 nautical miles, running conventional sail training programmes for disadvantaged and other young people and day-sails out of ports along the Belgian coast. She is operated as a non-profit enterprise and ongoing maintenance work continues to be undertaken by young volunteers under supervision.

Photos: (below) Pit de Jonge, (below right) Rupel Archive

National flag	Belgium
Home port	Boom
Sparred length	22.5 m
Rig	Gaff schooner
Sail area	200 sq m
Displacement	35 tons
Hull material	Wood
Owner/operator	t-groep
Built	Boom, Belgium
Launched	1996

W: www.rupel.be **E:** zeilschiprupel@gmail.be

NRP Sagres

A school ship for the Portuguese Navy since 1962, *Sagres* has an interesting history and pedigree. She was built in 1937 as a training ship for the German Navy, one of four identical ships built for this purpose – all taken by other countries as war reparations after World War II. *Sagres* (then the *Albert Leo Schlageter*) was captured by US forces in 1945 and handed on to Brazil in 1948. She was acquired by the Portuguese Navy in 1962 to replace another sail training tall ship (also named *Sagres*). Apart from two years for major refit work, she has sailed every year since then, visiting 60 countries and completing three circumnavigations as a roving ambassador for her country and the Portuguese Navy.

Photos: Sagres Archive

National flag	Portugal
Home port	Lisbon
Sparred length	89.5 m
Rig	Barque
Sail area	1,971 sq m
Gross tons	1,893
Hull material	Riveted steel
Owner/operator	Portuguese Navy
Built	Hamburg, Germany
Launched	1937

W sagres.marinha.pt E adj.rpublicas@marinha.pt

Santa Maria Manuela

Santa Maria Manuela was built in 1937 to fish for cod off the Grand Banks and Greenland. She was part of the famous Portuguese White Fleet. In 1993 she was declared obsolete, laid up and partially demolished. The Portuguese fishing and processing company Pascoal & Filhos acquired the hull and rebuilt the ship to her original traditional condition. In addition to sail training and team-building programmes, the vessel is used for a range of purposes, including tourism, bird and whale watching, scientific expeditions and astrological observation.

Photos: Santa Maria Manuela Archive

National flag	Portugal
Home port	Aveiro
Sparred length	68.64 m
Rig	Gaff schooner
Sail area	1,120 sq m
Gross tons	607
Hull material	Steel
Owner/operator	Pascoal & Filhos
Built	Lisbon, Portugal
Launched	1937 (relaunched 2010)

W www.santamariamanuela.pt
E santamariamanuela@gmail.com

Sedov

Built in 1921 for the German shipping company F A Vinnen as a freighter (the *Magdalene Vinnen I*), this ship traded initially between Europe and South America (saltpetre) and then between Europe and Australia (wheat). Ownership was eventually transferred to Britain in 1949 as war reparations and then to Russia, where she was renamed after Georgij J Sedov, a famous 19th-century Russian polar explorer. She is operated by the State Fishing Academy in Murmansk as a school ship, but she also sails with paying passengers.

National flag	Russia
Home port	Murmansk
Sparred length	117.50 m
Rig	Barque
Sail area	4,192 sq m
Gross tons	3,476
Hull material	Steel
Owner/operator	State Fishing Academy, Murmansk
Built	Kiel, Germany
Launched	1921

W www.sts-sedov.info **E** info@sts-sedov.info

Photos: Valery Vasilevskiy

RNOV Shabab Oman

This ship was built in 1971 as a sail training and expedition school ship for the UK's Dulverton Trust when she was named *Captain Scott* to revive the spirit and name of the Antarctic explorer Robert Falcon Scott. The Sultanate of Oman acquired her in 1977, renamed her *Shabab Oman* (Youth of Oman) and changed her rig from a schooner to a barquentine in 1984. *Shabab Oman* is operated by the Royal Navy of Oman and takes cadets from the military and police as well as civilian trainees nominated by the Ministry of Youth. Since 1987 she has competed in nine Tall Ships Races and won the coveted Friendship Trophy (see Chapter Four) on every occasion.

National flag	Sultanate of Oman
Home port	Muscat
Sparred length	52.10 m
Rig	Barquentine
Sail area	1,020 sq m
Gross tons	265
Hull material	Wood
Owner/operator	Royal Navy of Oman
Built	Buckie, Scotland
Launched	1971

W www.omanet.om/english/culture/shabab.asp
E shabab@skyfile.com

Photos: Royal Navy of Oman

Shtandart

The original *Shtandart* was the flagship of the first Russian fleet created by Peter the Great in the early 1700s. The current *Shtandart* is a replica, built in St Petersburg over a six-year period, mostly by young volunteers. Oak and larch trees were felled in the forests close to the city, then cut, shaped and assembled using equipment and methods modelled on 18th-century practices. Launched in 1998 by the UK's Prince Andrew and the Governor of St Petersburg (both Shtandart Project patrons), the ship sails mostly in the waters around Europe and is dedicated to sail training for the personal development of young people. The whole project has been managed from its conception by Vladimir Martus who is also the ship's captain.

National flag	Russia
Home port	St Petersburg
Sparred length	34.5 m
Rig	Full-rigged ship
Sail area	620 sq m
Gross tons	146
Hull material	Wood (oak and larch)
Owner/operator	Shtandart Project
Built	St Petersburg, Russia
Launched	1998

W www.shtandart.ru **E** question@shtandart.ru

Photos: (right) Vladimir Martus

Opposite page: (top left) Shtandart Archive
(top right) Vladimir Martus
(bottom) Alexander Lisafin

Simón Bolívar

One of four very similar barques built in Spain for Latin American navies, the *Simón Bolívar* is a cadet sail training ship and floating ambassador for Venezuela. She is named after the famous Venezuelan military and political leader in the early 1800s who is credited with liberating much of Latin America from Spanish domination. She undertakes one long training programme every year, enabling her to take part in many tall ship events around the world.

Photos: (below) Thad Koza, (below right top) Max Mudie, (below right bottom) Thad Koza

National flag	Venezuela
Home port	La Guaira
Sparred length	82.40 m
Rig	Barque
Sail area	1,650 sq m
Displacement	1,260 tons
Hull material	Steel
Owner/operator	Venezuelan Navy
Built	Bilbao, Spain
Launched	1979
W www.facebook.com/buqueescuelasimonbolivar	

Sørlandet

Funding from Norwegian ship owner Olaf Skjelbred enabled the construction of *Sørlandet* in 1927 as a sail training ship, mainly for 14- to 16-year-old cadets. At his insistence, she was built as a pure sailing ship with no engine (none was fitted until 1958). During World War II the ship was requisitioned by the occupying German forces and used to store coal, house German soldiers and as a prison. She had a major refit after the war and was returned to service as a sail training ship. A second major refit in 2012 restored her to her original condition, but with an engine. In addition to conventional sail training programmes for young people, *Sørlandet* undertakes charters for day-sails and longer voyages.

Photos: Sørlandet Archive

National flag	Norway
Home port	Oslo
Sparred length	65 m
Rig	Full-rigged ship
Sail area	1,236 sq m
Gross tons	499
Hull material	Riveted steel
Owner/operator	Stiftelsen Fullriggeren Sørlandet
Built	Kristiansand, Norway
Launched	1927

W www.fullriggeren-sorlandet.no
E post@fullriggeren-sorlandet.no

Spirit of Bermuda

The design of *Spirit of Bermuda*, purpose-built for youth development, was based on the schooners constructed by Bermudians, enslaved and free, in the 19th century. The Bermuda rig was developed for the sloops of the 17th to early 19th century for upwind short tacking around the island's coast and sailing to the fishing banks. To date, more than 3,500 young Bermudians (aged 12–25) have sailed on the vessel under programmes partially funded by the island's government and corporate donors. Most voyages are a structured five-day programme for school students, but many are for a wider age range and longer periods, including occasional passages to North America, the Caribbean and Europe.

National flag	Bermuda
Home port	Hamilton
Sparred length	35.97 m
Rig	Schooner
Sail area	455.92 sq m
Gross tons	92
Hull material	Wood (fibreglass-sheathed mahogany on Douglas fir)
Owner/operator	Bermuda Sloop Foundation
Built	Rockport, Maine, USA
Launched	2006

W www.bermudasloop.org **E** info@bermudasloop.org

Photos: (right) Alison Langley

Opposite page: (top) Alison Langley
(bottom) Charles Anderson

Spirit of New Zealand

Inspired by the 1960s renaissance of tall ships for youth development in the UK, the topsail schooner *Spirit of Adventure* was launched by philanthropist Lou Fisher in 1972. She was followed by the larger *Spirit of New Zealand* 14 years later and both operated successfully until *Spirit of Adventure* was decommissioned in 1997. About 70,000 trainees aged 15–18 from high schools around the country have sailed on ten-day voyages, mostly around the fabled Hauraki Gulf, with funding support from the Spirit of Adventure Trust, corporate sponsors and, only recently, government money. Voyage programmes are also run for naval midshipmen, disabled teens and school groups of 14-year-olds.

National flag	New Zealand
Home port	Auckland
Sparred length	45.2 m
Rig	Barquentine
Sail area	724.3 sq m
Gross tons	184
Hull material	Riveted steel
Owner/operator	Spirit of Adventure Trust
Built	Auckland, New Zealand
Launched	1986

W www.spiritofadventure.org.nz
E info@spiritofadventure.org.nz

Photos: Spirit of Adventure Trust Archive

St Lawrence II

Designed specifically as a sail training ship for young people, *St Lawrence II* was built in Kingston, Ontario, in the early 1950s. The finishing work and fit-out on her was undertaken by the Kingston Sea Cadets and enthusiastic amateurs, as well as local craftsmen. She was originally attached to the Royal Canadian Sea Cadets, but her programme was soon opened up to all 13- to 18-year-olds.

Photos: Chris Chafe

National flag	Canada
Home port	Kingston, Ontario
Sparred length	22.5 m
Rig	Brigantine
Sail area	240 sq m
Gross tons	35
Hull material	Steel
Owner/operator	Brigantine Inc
Built	Kingston, Ontario
Launched	1953

W www.brigantine.ca **E** info@brigantine.ca

Stad Amsterdam

The design of *Stad Amsterdam* was inspired by the 19th-century merchant clipper ship *De Amsterdam* of the East India Trading Company. The project to build the ship, launched in 2000, was the initiative of Dutch businessman Frits Goldschmeding working together with the Amsterdam city council. Completion and fit-out of the ship was undertaken at the Amsterdam Nautical History Museum to ensure authenticity.

Much of the project was completed by school-leavers and unemployed youth working under supervision. This too was an initiative of Goldschmeding, founder of the Randstad Holding employment agency. *Stad Amsterdam* serves as a sail training and passenger ship. In 2009 she undertook an eight-month circumnavigation as the star of a TV programme commemorating the 200th anniversary of Charles Darwin's birth.

Photos: Stad Amsterdam Archive

National flag	Netherlands
Home port	Amsterdam
Sparred length	76 m
Rig	Full-rigged ship
Sail area	2,200 sq m
Gross tons	698
Hull material	Steel
Owner/operator	Shipping company Clipper Stad Amsterdam
Built	Amsterdam, Netherlands
Launched	2000

W www.stadamsterdam.com E sales@stadamsterdam.nl

Statsraad Lehmkuhl

Statsraad Lehmkuhl is the oldest and largest of the three Norwegian tall ships. Launched in 1914 as a training ship for the German merchant marine, she was taken by the British as a war prize after World War I. A few years later, she was acquired by the Norwegian Ship Owners' Association under an initiative by Norwegian politician Kristofer Lehmkuhl. Apart from a period of confiscation by Germany during World War II, she has remained in Norwegian ownership as a sail training vessel. Her current owner, the Statsraad Lehmkuhl Foundation, which was created in 1978, runs independent voyages and charters for private individuals and groups, schools, companies and the Norwegian Naval Academy.

National flag	Norway 
Home port	Bergen
Sparred length	98 m
Rig	Square-rigged three-masted barque
Sail area	2,026 sq m
Gross tons	1,516
Hull material	Riveted steel
Owner/operator	Stiftelsen Seilskipet Statsraad Lehmkuhl
Launched	1914

W www.lehmkuhl.no **E** lehmkuhl@lehmkuhl.no

Photos: (right) Statsraad Lehmkuhl Foundation

Opposite page: (top left) Helen Wilgohs
(top right and bottom) Statsraad Lehmkuhl Foundation

INS Tarangini and INS Sudarshini

These two ships are virtually twins in terms of their dimensions, rig and purpose. Both are sail training ships for the Indian Navy. INS *Tarangini* (Waves) was commissioned in 1997 and INS *Sudarshini* (Beautiful Lady) in 2012. Year-round training programmes for officer cadets and ratings take place on both ships, mostly in the seas around India. However, since coming into service, INS *Tarangini* has sailed well over one million nautical miles with 13 major expeditions, including two circumnavigations with visits to 40 countries. On these expeditions she also served as an ambassador for India, promoting Indian culture and international friendship. The Indian Navy decided to commission a second training ship to cater for growth in the navy and as a reflection of its commitment to sail training.

Tarangini (T), Sudarshini (S)

National flag	India
Home port	Kochi
Sparred length	54 m
Rig	Barque
Sail area	965 sq m
Gross tons	517
Hull material	Steel
Owner/operator	Indian Navy
Built	Vasco da Gama, Goa, India
Launched	1995 (T), 2011 (S)
W	www.indiannavy.nic.in/naval-fleet/sail-training-ships

Photos: Indian Navy

Tecla

Owned and operated much of the year as a sail training vessel by the Bouwman-Sluik family, *Tecla* was launched in 1915 as a herring drifter working in the North Sea. She had no engine until the late 1920s when she was sold to a Danish owner who used her as a cargo vessel. *Tecla* returned to Dutch ownership in 1985, after a long period of being laid up, to be rebuilt and operated as a charter vessel. The Bouwman-Sluik family acquired her in 2006 and she completed a circumnavigation in 2014.

Photos: Tecla Archive

National flag	Netherlands
Home port	Den Helder
Sparred length	38 m
Rig	Gaff ketch
Sail area	370 sq m
Displacement	92 tons
Hull material	Steel
Owner/operator	Bouwman-Sluik
Built	Vlaardingen, Netherlands
Launched	1915

W www.tecla.nl **E** info@tecla.nl

Thalassa

In her first and fairly short life, this vessel was a fishing trawler. She was built in 1980 but foundered on a wreck just outside the harbour of Den Helder only five years later. She was salvaged and, ten years later, she was bought and rebuilt as a barquentine. She operates as a sail training vessel throughout much of the year, mainly in European waters, and as a charter vessel for day-sails and longer voyages.

Photos: (below) Xabier Armendarz, (below right) Silvester Kok

National flag	Netherlands
Home port	Harlingen
Sparred length	47 m
Rig	Barquentine
Sail area	800 sq m
Gross tons	257
Hull material	Steel
Owner/operator	Sailing Charter Thalassa
Built	Zaandam, Netherlands
Launched	1980

W www.tallshipthalassa.com **E** sail.thalassa@vaart.net

Thor Heyerdahl

Thor Heyerdahl was built in the Netherlands in 1930 as a single-masted cargo ship named *Tinka*, trading between Europe, Africa and the Caribbean. She underwent a major rebuild and relaunch in Germany in 1983 and now operates as a sail training ship throughout the year. The summer months are spent mostly in the North Sea and Baltic. In winter she undertakes voyages of six to seven months to South, Central and North America with secondary school pupils aged 15–17. During these passages normal school lessons take place combined with the sail training programme. The ship was renamed *Thor Heyerdahl* in 1981 by Detlef Soitzek, the initiator of the Thor Heyerdahl project and her first captain. In the late 1970s Soitzek had been the navigator for the Norwegian explorer Thor Heyerdahl's expedition on *Tigris*.

National flag	Germany
Home port	Kiel
Sparred length	49.83 m
Rig	Topsail schooner
Sail area	850 sq m
Gross tons	210
Hull material	Welded steel
Owner/operator	Segelschiff THOR HEYERDAHL gemeinnützige Fördergesellschaft
Built	Westerbroek, Netherlands (rebuilt Kiel, Germany)
Launched	1930 (relaunched 1983)

W www.thor-heyerdahl.de E mail@thor-heyerdahl.de

Photos: (right) Max Mudie

Opposite page: Thor Heyerdahl Archive

Tre Kronor af Stockholm

Tre Kronor af Stockholm was built to a design inspired by Scandinavian trading brigs of the mid 1800s for sail training and passenger/charter work. The ship's principal mission today is to promote sustainable development of the Baltic Sea through the Briggen Tre Kronor's Sustainable Seas Initiative. This involves scientists, non-governmental organisations, politicians and industry working together for a cleaner and healthier Baltic Sea. The project is supported by HRH Crown Princess Victoria who launched the ship in 2005.

Photos: Per Björkdahl

National flag	Sweden
Home port	Stockholm
Sparred length	45 m
Rig	Brig
Sail area	750 sq m
Gross tons	191
Hull material	Wood (oak)
Owner/operator	Briggen Tre Kronor
Built	Stockholm, Sweden
Launched	2005

W www.briggentrekronor.se **E** info@briggentrekronor.se

Tunas Samudera

The design and build of *Tunas Samudera* was jointly funded by the British and Malaysian governments. She was handed over to the Malaysian Navy in 1989 in a joint ceremony by Her Majesty Queen Elizabeth II and His Majesty Yang Di-Pertuan Agong. The ship is operated as a sail training vessel by the Royal Malaysian Navy, but training voyages are run for civilian youth groups as well as navy cadets. Her name means 'Offspring of the Ocean'. She is a sister ship to the Australian Navy's *Young Endeavour*, which was built in the same yard two years earlier.

Photos: (below) Herbert H Boehm, (below right) Max Mudie

National flag	Malaysia
Home port	Lumut Perak
Sparred length	44 m
Rig	Brigantine
Sail area	569 sq m
Gross tons	173
Hull material	Steel
Owner/operator	Royal Malaysian Navy
Built	Lowestoft, UK
Launched	1989
W www.navy.mil.my	

Vera Cruz

An exact replica of the Portuguese caravels that sailed the Atlantic Ocean in the 15th century, *Vera Cruz* is the third caravel built and operated by Aporvela, the Portuguese Sail Training Association. She serves as a sail training ship, mostly for young people, but is also used for research and scientific programmes with Portuguese universities. More than 100,000 school children have visited the ship since her launch in 2001 as part of the association's school field trip programmes.

National flag	Portugal
Home port	Vila do Conde
Sparred length	23.82 m
Rig	Caravel
Sail area	760 sq m
Gross tons	86
Hull material	Wood
Owner/operator	Aporvela (Portuguese Sail Training Association)
Built	Vila do Conde, Portugal
Launched	2001
W www.aporvela.pt **E** geral@aporvela.pt	

Photos: Aporvela

Windeward Bound

Thirty years elapsed between the original idea and the launch of *Windeward Bound* in 1996. The dream was to build and operate a ship like the *New Endeavour*, a Baltic trader that arrived in Sydney from the UK in 1965. When that ship was broken up in 1987, her masts, yards, anchor gear and some of her sails were saved to be incorporated into the build of *Windeward Bound*. The ship's design was based on the detailed plans for a topsail schooner dating from 1848 unearthed from the Smithsonian Institution in the US. She was built in Hobart over five years, mainly by volunteers. These included a growing number of disadvantaged youth. Providing the sail training experience for this section of society (as well as the wider community) became the main focus of the Windeward Bound Trust, created to operate the ship.

Photos: Windeward Bound Trust

National flag	Australia
Home port	Hobart, Tasmania
Sparred length	33 m
Rig	Brigantine
Sail area	355 sq m
Gross tons	100
Hull material	Wood (mountain ash)
Owner/operator	Sarah Parry and others/ The Windeward Bound Trust
Built	Hobart, Tasmania
Launched	1996

W www.windewardbound.com
E windbound5@bigpond.com

Wylde Swan

The largest two-masted topsail schooner in the world, *Wylde Swan* was designed and built for high performance both in terms of speed and as a platform for sail training. As evidence of this, in her first season of operation she was first overall and first in class in the Tall Ships Races 2011 and winner of the coveted Friendship Trophy. She conducts conventional sail training programmes during the summer months in European waters. In winter she sails with high school students and teachers to the Caribbean, with an educational programme focusing on science, exploration and personal development.

Photos: Arthur op Zee

National flag	Netherlands
Home port	Makkum
Sparred length	62 m
Rig	Topsail schooner
Sail area	1,130 sq m
Gross tons	269
Hull material	Iron
Owner/operator	Hinke de Vries and Jurgens Hanekom
Built	Makkum, Netherlands
Launched	2010

W www.wyldeswan.eu **E** info@wyldeswan.eu

STS Young Endeavour

Australia's national sail training ship, the *Young Endeavour*, was a bicentennial gift from the UK, dedicated 'to the benefit of the young people of Australia'. She sailed from the UK in 1987 with a crew of young people, arriving in Sydney in time for bicentennial celebrations the following year. Since then, more than 11,000 young Australians (aged 16–23) have participated in sail training voyages, completing the Young Endeavour Youth Development Program, and another 10,000 young people have taken part in the ship's day-sail programme (which has a particular focus on those with special needs). The *Young Endeavour* operates mostly on the east coast of Australia, but has circumnavigated the country twice and sailed around the world once.

National flag	Australia
Home port	Sydney
Sparred length	44 m
Rig	Brigantine
Sail area	740.6 sq m
Gross tons	175
Hull material	Steel
Owner/operator	Royal Australian Navy
Built	Lowestoft, UK
Launched	1987

W www.youngendeavour.gov.au
E mail@youngendeavour.gov.au

Photos: Young Endeavour Youth Scheme

Zawisza Czarny II

The world's biggest sail training ship of the scouting movement, *Zawisza Czarny II* was built in 1952 as a fishing vessel. She was rebuilt and converted to a sail training ship in 1961, replacing the Polish Scouts vessel *Zawisza Czarny I*, which had sunk in 1949. She is named after a Polish folk hero, a medieval black knight and symbol of loyalty and reliability. *Zawisza Czarny II* achieved international fame in 1984 when she stood by to rescue survivors from the sinking *Marques* during a violent storm near Bermuda.

Photos: (below) Wojciech Miloch, (below right top) Max Mudie, (below right bottom) Tomasz Maracewicz

National flag	Poland
Home port	Gdynia
Sparred length	42.7 m
Rig	Staysail schooner
Sail area	439 sq m
Gross tons	164
Hull material	Steel
Owner/operator	Polish Scouting and Guiding Association
Built	Gdansk, Poland
Launched	1952

W www.zawiszaczarny.pl
E cwm@zhp.pl

Zénobe Gramme

Named after the Belgian inventor of the dynamo, Zénobe Théophile Gramme, the ship was built in 1961 for the Belgian Navy to serve as an oceanographic research vessel. In 1970 she became a sail training ship mainly for Belgian Navy cadets, but also for young civilians, and to represent the country at international maritime events. Since being commissioned she has sailed more than 350,000 nautical miles.

Photos: (below) Belgian Ministry of Defence, (below right) Max Mudie

National flag	Belgium
Home port	Zeebrugge
Sparred length	29 m
Rig	Bermudian ketch
Sail area	700 sq m
Gross tons	136
Hull material	Steel
Owner/operator	Belgian Ministry of Defence
Built	Temse, Belgium
Launched	1961
W www.mil.be/navycomp	
E zenobegramme.A.mil.be	

NIGEL ROWE

THE TALL SHIP EXPERIENCE

CHANGING YOUNG PEOPLE'S LIVES

3

Photo: Tall Ships America

Robert had not been to sea before. Not ever, even in a small boat. So his decision to undertake a voyage on a tall ship as one of the trainee crew was a big one, and somewhat surprising as he was a quiet young man who had had little adventure in his life. He was persuaded to take the plunge by one of his school friends, Paula, who had sailed as a trainee in a tall ships race the year before. 'Go on,' she said. 'It'll change your life, I promise. It's not really about learning to sail a tall ship, although that's very interesting, it's what you learn about yourself and life that got me hooked!'

Robert thought it sounded like a fun adventure and, as he was about to have his 18th birthday, now seemed like a good time to do something different.

He had never actually seen a tall ship before, other than in photographs. So when he arrived at the dockside he just stared open-mouthed at the sheer size of the vessel. Most of all, he marvelled at the height of the masts because he knew climbing them would be something he might have the opportunity to do.

STEPPING ON BOARD

Robert walked up the gangway unsteadily with his bag over his shoulder, wondering what he had got himself into. He was met at the top by one of the ship's officers and taken below to his bunk. There would be 36 trainees, each with their own bunk along the port and starboard sides of the ship. There would be an almost equal number of young women and men as it turned out, most between 16 and 25 years old. It was early afternoon, he was one of the last trainees to arrive and it soon became clear there was a lot that had to be done and learned in the next few hours. The captain had decided to leave that evening and motor-sail to an anchorage in a quiet cove a couple of hours down the coast for the night.

Everyone crowded into the saloon to meet and be briefed on the voyage plan – the 36 trainees, four older volunteer watch leaders and nine permanent professional crew. It was a tight squeeze.

The captain introduced the other professional

Photos: (this page and opposite) Herbert H Boehm

crew and the four watch leaders. There would be four groups of nine trainees, each watch on duty for a few hours twice in a 24-hour cycle so that everyone would have the experience of sailing the ship during the night as well as the day. The captain explained the voyage plan he had in mind and the weather forecast that helped to determine it. While they would be at sea almost all of the time in the coming ten days, short visits to a couple of ports were planned. This brought smiles and a cheer from the trainees.

Safety equipment and drills dominated the rest of the briefing before the trainees were told who else would be in their watch and who their watch leader would be. Everyone would be expected to participate fully in running the ship, they were told, but no one would be expected to do anything that wasn't safe. All the trainees were given a logbook to record the elements of the training programme they completed successfully. Robert thumbed through it. But, before that first day ended, it became pretty clear that the adventure was going to be about a whole lot more than safety and seamanship!

There were four other boys in Robert's watch and four girls. Up on deck after the briefing, their watch leader, a cheerful man in his late 20s who had sailed on the ship a few times in the past, handed out foul-weather clothing, life jackets and harnesses. He walked them round the deck, explaining what they would have to do during a watch at sea. Robert soon lost track of what purpose each of the bewildering array of ropes served. Then came the challenge he had hoped for but also dreaded. Each trainee was asked if they would like to go aloft, climb the mast and perhaps also go out on the yards. Robert was the first to put his hand up.

GOING ALOFT

Because this was his first time doing it, the ship's mate went ahead of him and his watch leader went behind him. With every step he took up the ratlines, the

more nervous he began to feel as he climbed further and further from the deck. It was a slow climb, with the really testing task to come as he reached the first platform almost 12 metres above the deck. He watched the mate ahead of him climb out on the futtock shrouds and over the lip of the platform. Robert clenched his teeth, clipped his harness to the shrouds and clambered on to the platform himself, short of breath, his legs shaking, his hands aching and white-knuckled from gripping the handholds so tightly. This was without doubt the scariest thing he had ever done in his life. He stood on the platform with the mate and his watch leader. The other trainees in his watch down on the deck gave him a loud cheer. He felt fantastic.

Robert was keen to see what it was like out on the yards, and the mate and watch leader agreed. Again the mate went first and Robert followed closely, copying everything the mate did. He clipped his harness to the steel wire that ran the length of the yard and carefully stepped on to the foot rope that hung about a metre below. Holding on to the rail with both hands he slowly moved out along the yard, sliding his feet sideways along the foot rope. It was easier than he thought it would be, but he wondered how it would feel doing it at sea, with the ship rolling and having the task of letting the huge square sails go or furling them in. But that, he said to himself, was for another day.

Despite the confidence his adventure up the mast had given him, Robert felt anxiety as well as excitement as the ship left the dock under engine. It was all so new and somewhat daunting, not least the prospect of having to work as a team with people he didn't know, wondering how much of a fool he was going to make of himself. He felt completely isolated, particularly as he, along with all the other trainees, had had to hand over his passport, money and mobile phone to the mate for safe keeping. He couldn't remember the last time he had been separated from his phone and he felt lost without it!

Photo: Herbert H Boehm

Soon after leaving the harbour the ship was steered to a course away from the wind, orders were given and there was a flurry of activity. Although the ship would rely principally on her engine for the short passage to the anchorage, the captain had decided to set some sail. The wind was light and he wanted the new trainees to see a little more of how things worked on board. The lower sails were unfurled on the foremast and the trainees on deck hauled on the lines to set them square to the wind. Robert leaned against the guard rail by the bridge and just smiled. A cocktail of nervousness and excitement swept through him. The question was, would he be up to what would be demanded of him when it was his turn to be on watch?

Everyone including Robert had a massive appetite for breakfast the following morning with all the fresh air and excitement. Then it was up on deck again for a final run through the ship's operation and safety drills before the anchor was hauled up, the sails were set and the voyage proper was under way.

It was amazing to Robert how quickly the nine strangers in his watch gelled together under the guidance and leadership of their watch leader. The imperative of things having to be done quickly and in the right sequence by those out on the yards furling or setting the sails, those on deck heaving or slackening the lines that alter the angle of the sails and the person on the wheel steering the course quickly became very clear. These tasks would be more difficult at night, of course, and more difficult still in rough weather.

STORMY WEATHER

Three days into the voyage the wind began to stiffen, and the sea became more unsettled, buffeting the hull and causing the ship to roll and judder. Not everyone succumbed to seasickness by any means, but it was not long before Robert felt his stomach beginning to churn, particularly when one of his watch mates began to throw up over the side of the ship. Robert decided to stay on deck and not let seasickness get

Photo: Stine Tanderup Pedersen

the better of him. By the time the sun was setting he felt he had conquered it, but this was not the case for everyone on board. A few were below tucked up and groaning, with a bucket next to their bunks.

As the sun began to dip below the horizon the wind continued to rise and whistle in the rigging. The captain decided to shorten sail. Robert was among the trainees who volunteered to go aloft. This would be his first time in such conditions. The ship was rising, falling and rolling in the heavy seas. Under the watchful eye of the mate and the watch leader, he clipped on his harness, climbed the ratlines to the second platform, then out on to the yard, while others climbed higher still to the next set of yards. Almost 18 metres above the deck where Robert was, the movement of the ship was much more violent and he gripped the steel wire along the top of the yard so tightly his hands began to hurt. But he and the others soon had the big sails furled and secured before their slow descent to the deck. He felt heroic!

At home Robert always needed a full night's sleep and found it difficult to get out of bed in the morning. But here, on a tall ship at sea, he loved it when he was on watch at night. He had never seen the sky so black or the stars so bright and so many more of them than he ever knew there were. The sound of the wind in the sails and the ship moving through the water was different at night, too, louder somehow, energising and quite mystical.

It was not long before Robert's confidence began to grow as he learned more about the ship's operation and began to get a grip on all the essential tasks that kept the ship going. He had several sessions in the wheelhouse and the privilege of actually steering the ship. Albeit under the watchful eye of the mate, it gave him a sense of power and responsibility he had not experienced before. He also worked on the charts with one of the other officers to calculate the distance, course and time to their next waypoint and the port where they would have a few hours ashore.

Photos: (this page and opposite) Stine Tanderup Pedersen

All these tasks were entirely new to him, both fascinating and rewarding. For one thing, it brought to life some of the things he had learned in maths, physics and IT lessons that he had never seen the relevance of before.

CONFIDENCE AND AMBITION

The social life on board became an important part of the voyage experience, too. All the trainees took turns to clean the ship, help prepare the meals in the galley and clear up afterwards, and there were plenty of other times to get to know each other, relaxing in the saloon playing cards, reading or just chatting. There were five other nationalities in the trainee crew, all from different backgrounds, each with a different and interesting perspective on life. The two short trips ashore were further opportunities to develop friendships and share the new experience and freedom without the demands of helping to run the ship.

The ten-day voyage was over too soon for Robert and for most of the rest of the trainee crew. By the end of it they were all very familiar with the on-board tasks, most had completed the training course satisfactorily, many had had the unforgettable experience of climbing aloft and only a few had succumbed to the horrors of seasickness. Members of Robert's watch had all exchanged contact details and all but the boy who had spent half the voyage in his bunk with seasickness said they hoped they would have the opportunity to sail together again next year.

When he walked down the gangway to leave for home, Robert cast his mind back to the day he had climbed nervously aboard the ship. He felt a different person now. He had done things he never dreamed he could, let alone would. He felt more self-confident and more ambitious for his future. For one thing, the captain had told him that with another voyage under his belt he would have the potential to be a watch leader. He had forged several new friendships with people he knew he would stay in touch with. Living and working together in relative isolation and at such close quarters, they now felt like 'family'. He began to think that perhaps the whole experience had, as his friend Paula back home had said it would, changed his life. Although it would be more accurate, he thought, to say it had given him the self-assurance and ability to change his life himself – to be in the driving seat, to think differently and with broader horizons about what mattered to him as a person and what he wanted to do with his life.

Photos: (top) Picton Castle Archive
(above) Arwen Bijker
(right) Rienk Boode

Opposite page: (top left) At Sea Sail Training
(top right) Valery Vasilevskiy
(bottom) Montenegro Navy

THE VALUE AND POWER OF SAIL TRAINING

Robert's experience on a tall ship is quite common. There is now a wealth of independent research to validate the extraordinary power of sail training on a tall ship, particularly for the young (see www.sailtraininginternational.org/vessels/research).

The value and power of sail training derives from its unique combination of characteristics: the mastering of new and complex practical skills during an intensive programme of experiential learning over an extended period of time in an unfamiliar and sometimes hostile environment. Although it is clearly an attraction for many, learning to sail is not the essential goal of sail training. Nor is it just an opportunity for an adventure. But these characteristics are key to the main purposes and value of the sail training experience.

An unavoidable and planned purpose of sail training is to give young people what are known today as 'social and employability skills'. These include an understanding of, and the skills required for, teamwork and leadership, as well as improved self-confidence and the basic disciplines and inter-personal skills that help to ensure a well-balanced life in society. Personal health and well-being are an important part of the mix, too. So is the encouragement it gives young trainees to reflect on and explore their personal values and potential.

EXPERIENTIAL LEARNING

So what is so special about experiential learning and what are the unique strengths of sail training in this context?

Put simply, the power of experiential learning is that it unites theory and practice. For fairly obvious reasons it is an entirely different learning experience to that available in a classroom or from a book. It is essentially about watching and learning from people who know what they're doing when actually performing a task and then putting it into practice oneself. The experience is intensified when it takes place in an unfamiliar environment and over an extended and concentrated period of time (i.e. not just an afternoon or a few days), when it involves the acquisition of new skills (particularly when these are unrelated to a person's normal day-to-day life) and when working as a team is absolutely essential to getting anything done. Climbing mountains and trekking across deserts or through jungles are among the outdoor adventure activities that use the basic building blocks of effective experiential learning and achieve some of these things. They all involve the acquisition and mastery of new skills in an unfamiliar environment. But sail training adds extraordinarily valuable elements to these basic building blocks in a more complete package that is unique to, or particularly prominent in, a training voyage on a tall ship.

A number of sail training programmes run for several weeks or even a few months. But the majority by far run over one to two weeks, a period of time that is practical for any individual and very effective in delivering the benefits of the sail training experience. A voyage at sea on a tall ship is a round-the-clock activity that involves everyone on board in a virtuous circle of experience: learning and practising complex new skills, reflecting on them and discussing them with other trainees and the professional crew, then repeating them in different conditions, both during the day and at night.

Teamwork and effective leadership are essential, not just desirable, to the running of a sailing ship. This is not only about safety and the practice of good seamanship. Without teamwork and leadership, the vessel is simply not going to function. For example, altering course on a tall ship requires very precise co-ordination of a number of component tasks in the space of just a few minutes: steering to the new course, perhaps furling or setting some of the sails from the yards immediately before doing so, moving all the sails, probably a dozen or more of them, through a wide angle to keep them full as the ship alters course, then fine-tuning the set of the sails to squeeze the maximum power from the wind before securing the lines on deck. Even those below deck need to be involved when this is happening because the movement of the ship and her angle of heel can affect everything and everyone on board. There are very few activities in any sphere where teamwork and leadership are more vital to the accomplishment of a task.

Living and working alongside other people of different backgrounds and abilities in a relatively small 'home', isolated from the familiarities of life on dry land, adds a level of intensity. The experience of climbing a mast and setting sails, chart work and steering the ship, understanding the powerful forces of nature at work at sea – all these things, the mastering of new and unfamiliar skills and technologies, help to build self-confidence and a sense of self-worth. This issue of self-confidence is particularly interesting. There are many activities and experiences in life that can build a person's self-confidence, but often this comes with a number of negative side effects (increased aggression, risky attitudes, even racial, class or gender bias). Studies have shown that the sail training experience has a positive impact on self-confidence that endures over time without facilitating these negative side effects. In fact, the sail training experience is a great leveller. It builds confidence and self-assurance, but it also challenges the more overbearing and arrogant.

On many sail training voyages there will be trainees from a wide range of backgrounds. A few ships are able to cater for the needs of people of mixed ability. Unique among them are the two ships operated by the UK's Jubilee Sailing Trust (see page 106). On many ships, particularly those in Europe, there will be trainees from a number of different countries and cultures. All these factors also play into the unique package of values and benefits inherent in the sail training experience on a tall ship. Cross-cultural education and understanding has a growing importance in an increasingly globalised world.

DEVELOPING 'BEST PRACTICE'

A number of schemes and programmes have been introduced over the past decade to promote best practice in key aspects of training programmes, on-board safety and protection of the marine environment. Details on those that follow here are available on the Sail Training International website (www.sailtraininginternational.org).

PROGRAMME CONTENT AND VALIDATION

The international tall ship fleet is very diverse in terms of heritage, size and rig, and at-sea experience. Add to this the considerable differences in national cultures and the personality of those engaged in ship management, notably the captain and chief mate, and it is not surprising that sail training programmes also differ from ship to ship. But the basic elements of what constitutes an effective sail training experience are better understood these days and are widely shared as best practice. A great deal of work has been done over the past several years to achieve this through the 53-page Sail Training International *Programme Evaluation Self-Assessment Toolkit*. This comprehensive manual was developed by Sail Training International in collaboration with Dr Kris Von Wald of Learning and Change Consulting and Dr Pete Allison of the University of Edinburgh and in consultation with a wide range of tall ship operators around the world.

TRAINEE LOGBOOK

That a sail training ship should have an effective training programme and be able to validate such a claim is clearly important to trainees and to those who help fund their participation. It is also important for trainees to leave the ship at the end of a voyage with confirmation of the training programme they have completed. Based on the above work on programme content, Sail Training International introduced its trainee logbook, a record of basic safety and seamanship training. It is regarded by many as the gold standard for basic training programmes and is used by many ships around the world. A number of ship operators also have their own trainee logbooks based on the specific programmes they provide.

SAFETY MANAGEMENT SYSTEM

It will be clear from the above that safety is a critical component of every aspect of on-board life for the trainee. But this goes beyond considerations relating to what a trainee is called upon to do. It applies to the overall organisation and management of a training ship to ensure the highest safety standards for the ship, those on board and the marine environment. Virtually all ships over 500 tons are required to comply with the International Maritime Organization's International Safety Management (ISM) Code covering these aspects with an audit and certification process operated by flag state authorities. Sail Training International has embraced the concept and philosophy of the ISM Code and developed a version of it specifically for sailing ships under 500 tons. This work was a collaboration with the Canadian Maritime Group and Dutch maritime consultancy Rood Boven Groen. The system, known as 'ISM Lite' and covered in a 54-page manual, was piloted in 2010–2011 and introduced for use by sail training tall ships in 2012.

BLUE FLAG SCHEME

Sail training tall ships have a natural affinity with the marine environment and its protection. They use the cleanest of all energy sources, the wind, for propulsion. The young people who sail on them tend to be more conscious than most of the need to take care of our seas. Sail Training International and the Foundation for Environmental Education have been natural partners in developing and promoting the increasingly popular Sail Training International Blue Flag Scheme in the tall ship fleet. Participating ships and those who sail on them sign up to a code of conduct relating to the discharge of waste, disturbance of marine animals and seabirds and fishing practices. Ships signed up to the scheme are issued with a special flag to signify their participation (see opposite page).

CAREERS AT SEA

This chapter has focused primarily on the tall ship experience for young people in general, and some of the structures and programmes in place to ensure trainees have a valuable and safe experience. But sail training on a tall ship is not just for those with an adventurous spirit seeking new experiences. It is also a key element of the training programme for young people seeking a career at sea. As will have been obvious from a review of the ships illustrated in Chapter Two, there are many tall ships owned or chartered by naval academies around the world, both merchant and military. These programmes involve considerably more time at sea and a much more broadly based curriculum.

Understanding the forces of nature at work at sea is important and interesting for anyone on a tall ship voyage, but it is critical to anyone who will earn their living at sea, probably on a large motorised ship with stabilisers and not much need to go out on deck in bad weather. Teamwork and leadership are also critical components in the running of any ship, whatever her size or method of propulsion.

Most naval academies around the world, merchant and military, have a long history of incorporating sail training as a critical component of their broader cadet training programmes. The US Coast Guard is a good example of this, operating the barque *Eagle* (see page 60) since 1946. Former *Eagle* captain Eric C Jones is eloquent on the subject, and his views are widely shared:

Sail Training International's ISM Lite manual, Self-Assessment Toolkit and Trainee Logbook. **Photo:** Max Mudie

Sail training is a crucial element of the programme run by the Coast Guard to prepare cadets for what is expected of them in the service. In fact, sailing on Eagle provides some elements of the broader training programme that is simply not available on any other type of vessel. It is a truly unique and challenging experience. Cadets understand discipline from very early on; but there is literally nothing like sailing on a tall ship to acquire an appreciation of why teamwork and leadership are so critical and what these concepts demand of an individual. On a sailing ship you also feel nature at work in a very real and usually very memorable sense, for example working aloft in foul weather. Just about every cadet who has sailed on Eagle will attest to the power and worth of the experience and the Coast Guard has a good deal of robust evidence of the effectiveness of sail training in the development of practical maritime skills.

Dr Henryk Sniegocki, master mariner and Deputy Rector for Maritime Affairs at the Gdynia Maritime University in Poland, which operates the Dar Młodzieży (see page 56), takes a similar line:

Training young men and women on tall ships is simply an indispensable element in educating future officers for the merchant fleet. It is very often the first and most important test of their suitability for the job, allowing them to confront their own vision of service at sea with genuine challenges. It brings the student as close as possible to the kind of problems that a future officer will have to face during a maritime career. Hard physical work shapes people's characters and sense of personal responsibility, creating habits essential for future service at sea. The need to work as a team is essential to the basic functioning of the ship and the safety of fellow crew members. High up, on the ship's masts or yards, acting together and thinking of others is essential. Very often the safety of friends depends on one's own actions, leaving no room for carelessness. Simulators are essential tools in the training of future officers, of course, but working with 'virtual' wind and sea has to be supplemented by genuine exposure to the elements and decisions made under real conditions: the best way to experience this is on board a sailing ship. Furthermore, the impact of a voyage under sail remains with you forever. It is often the most memorable time of one's entire career at sea!

Sail Training International's Blue Flag Scheme flag. **Photo:** Sail Training International

Photos: (top) Sail Training International
(above) Valery Vasilevskiy
(right) Sail Training International

Opposite page: (top) Marieke de Mink
(bottom) Valery Vasilevskiy

RON DADSWELL

RACING ON TALL SHIPS
INTERNATIONAL COMPETITION AND CULTURAL EXCHANGE

4

Racing takes the tall ship and sail training experience into the uniquely challenging environment of friendly competition and cultural exchange. The international tall ships races and regattas organised by Sail Training International and its member country organisations enable ships of different sizes and heritages to race on equal terms. They bring together young people of many different countries, cultures, backgrounds and abilities to share the experience and promote international friendship and understanding. They provide a spectacle and festive atmosphere for the many hundreds of thousands, sometimes more than a million, of visitors to each host port when the fleet is in. It is these events, more than any other activity, that earned Sail Training International its nomination for the Nobel Peace Prize 2007.

The races and regattas organised by Sail Training International are regarded by many as the charity's most valuable contribution to sail training for young people. They are certainly the highlight of the sailing year for many tall ships. The first ever Tall Ships Race took place between Torbay (UK) and Lisbon (Portugal) in 1956. Today the races take place

(below) The crew of the *Moyan* before the start of the first tall ships race in 1956
(next page) Some of the ships that took part in the first race moored in the River Dart, Torbay (UK) before the start
Photos: Sail Training International

annually in the seas around Europe and North America, and occasionally elsewhere in the world. The first race in 1956 had an entry of just 20 ships. Today's races sometimes attract a fleet of more than 100 vessels from around the world, with several thousand young trainees from 30 or more countries. The races are 'friendly' competitions but keenly contested.

Racing as part of a large fleet of vessels is a unique experience that inspires trainees to do their utmost to achieve a good placing and perhaps a prize. The races also provide the opportunity for participating port cities to showcase themselves to an international audience. The presence of a tall ships fleet can attract many hundreds of thousands of additional visitors to the city. The economic impact for local businesses is generally about ten times the investment.

The port visit at the end of a race usually lasts four days. There is an intense programme of activities for the crews, including inter-ship sporting competitions, the very colourful crew parade, the prize-giving and crew party. These events are opportunities for the young trainees to mix with those they have been competing against.

RACE PLANNING

The Tall Ships Races provide an incredible visual spectacle for the public and an unforgettable experience for the participants. The smoothness and success of a race series belies the massive amount of very detailed planning and management by Sail Training International's highly experienced event organisers and those in the port management teams.

The annual European series of races is organised on a four-year planning cycle so that each year the races take place in different parts of Europe, from the Baltic to the Bay of Biscay and beyond. In addition to the main annual European Tall Ships series, Sail Training International organises occasional transatlantic races and regattas in other sea areas such as the Mediterranean, Black Sea and, very occasionally, the Asia/Pacific region.

A similar procedure is followed in North America. Tall Ships America organises an annual 'Tall Ships Challenge' series of races, switching between the Atlantic and Pacific coasts and the Great Lakes. In addition the Canadian Sail Training Association is increasingly involved in organising events in its territorial waters. These races and events are in an important element in the calendar for sail trainers in the US and Canada. While the majority of entries are from these two countries, North American events also attract vessels from around the world. These races are run using the Sail Training International racing and sailing rules and time correction factor (TCF) which enable large square-rigged ships to race on an equal footing with smaller modern sailing vessels.

When selecting ports for the race circuit, whether in Europe or North America, there is always a wish to include suitable ports that have not hosted a race visit before and to reward those ports that have done so successfully. It is also ideal to include a mixture of large and small ports, particularly capital cities or cities that have some other attraction such as being the Capital of Culture for the year in question.

Another important factor is rewarding ports that support sail training for young people every year and not just in the year they are bidding to be a host port. There is a growing number of ports that have risen to this challenge and raise funds to help a number of their local youngsters take part in the races or other sail training voyages each year.

Where possible, Sail Training International will organise a 'chain' of events during the year so that there are races or regattas before and after the main summer series. A relatively recent example was the Garibaldi Tall Ships Regatta from Genoa in Italy to Trapani in Sicily, which was held in April and celebrated the 150th anniversary of Giuseppe Garibaldi unifying Italy and Sicily. The fleet then continued westward in the Mediterranean to the Historical Seas Tall Ships Regatta, a race from the Greek port of Volos to the Black Sea port of Varna in Bulgaria and then back to Istanbul, Turkey, before racing to Lavrion in Greece. This regatta in May was timed to allow the fleet to return to northern Europe by July to take part in the annual Tall Ships Races series, which started in Antwerp, Belgium.

This chain of events enabled vessels to take part in an attractive programme of port visits, races and regattas, with free berthing and crew programmes which stretched over more than six months.

Photos: (top) Sagres Archive
(above) Lauri Rotko
(right) Sail Training International

PORT PROGRAMME

Although hostage to wind and weather, race passages are planned so that the slowest vessels in the fleet should be able to arrive in port by midday on the first day of a four-day stopover. The aim is to leave about midday on the fourth day, but again this is subject to all manner of local considerations, including the weather and the tides.

In between arrival and departure there is a very full programme of activities arranged for the trainees and the ships' professional crews. It is important that the crews who have just raced enjoy the post-race events, which have been organised with them in mind, and that the new crews have the opportunity to get off to a good start with events that enable them to mix and bond quickly with their new friends.

It is a very busy and exciting time for the ships' professional crews who will be preparing for the next race with a crew of new trainees, many of whom will be local youngsters funded by the city to take part. Trying to fit in the safety briefings and training with the port programme can be a challenge but is all part of the intense and exciting build-up to the main event.

In addition to the 'highlight' events such as the crew parade, prize-giving and crew party, the port committee organises inter-ship sporting competitions and cultural visits to local places of interest.

The ports also organise a 'Crew Centre' where there are computer terminals, refreshments, table games and opportunity for the crews from many different countries and cultures to meet each other. Those who have just finished a race will have formed a strong 'family' bond with their shipmates and will also want to meet up with friends they have made on competing ships. The crew centre provides a social hub and plays an important part in enabling these meetings to take place.

In addition to the programme for the crews, the ports also have to invest in putting on an attractive programme of events that will entertain the many thousands of visitors who come to see the tall ships. These vary but almost always include open-air concerts and spectacular firework displays which both the crews and the visitors enjoy.

The visitors have to be accommodated and fed and they may want to take away a souvenir of their visit. This is where the local hotels, restaurants and traders benefit. Each port will carry out an economic impact study and they generally show at least a tenfold return on the investment required to stage the event.

For the host port the visit is an opportunity to bring local people together and to involve many of them as volunteers with a great pride in their city and a desire to make the visit a great success, not just for the crews and visitors, but also for tourism and local businesses.

Photos: (top left) Sztuczne Ognie and The Tall Ships Races 2013 Szczecin, (top right) Sail Training International, (bottom) The Tall Ships Races 2013 Szczecin
Next page: Adam Nurkiewicz

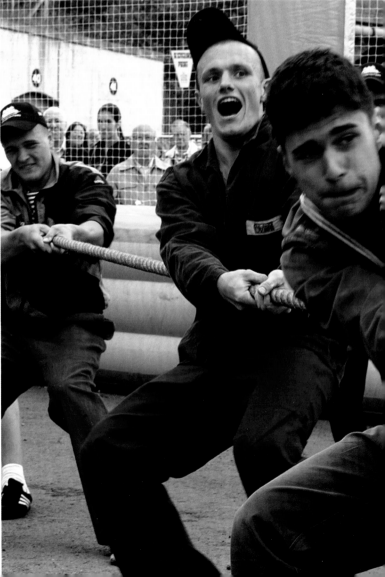

Photos: (top) Sail Training International
(above) Maurycy Śmierzchalski
(right) Sail Training International

Opposite page: (top) Lauri Rotko
(bottom) Sail Training International

ROYALTY AND HEADS OF STATE

From the first race in 1956 to the present time, members of European royal families and international heads of state have been closely involved with the tall ships races. In 1956 the race was started by the Patron, His Royal Highness Prince Philip, the Duke of Edinburgh. Other Patrons of the first race included the President of the French Republic, the President of Portugal, the King of Spain and the King of Belgium.

Prince Philip returned in 2006 to meet the trainees and to start the 50th anniversary race (photo top right) from almost the same start line as that used in 1956.

Almost every year the European races receive a visit from members of the royal family or the head of state of a country hosting the race. Usually this will include visits to sail training ships to meet the young trainee crew members. For example, during The Tall Ships Race visit to St Petersburg, Russia in 2009 President Putin (photo top left) showed his support for Sail Training International by presenting the prizes and making a speech on the value and importance of sail training; in 2010 Crown Princess Mette-Marit of Norway, as Royal Patron, attended the opening ceremony in Kristiansand, and she and Crown Prince Haakon invited trainees from each ship to a reception at their summer residence (photo bottom right); and Andris Berzins, President of Latvia (centre of photo, bottom) visited a number of vessels before officiating at the Parade of Sail out of Riga prior to the start of the last leg of the 2013 Tall Ships Races.

Photos: (top) Sail Training International, (right) Toms Kalnins **Opposite page:** Sail Training International

CREW PARADE

Those who have just raced have the opportunity to let their hair down during the crew parade through the city. This is a colourful event where the young crews try to outdo each other in their inventiveness in trying to produce costumes from what is available on board their ship. There is much dancing and singing during the parade, which is often enhanced with local bands and majorettes. The local port committee will provide a number of inducements in the way of prizes for the best-dressed crews or most enthusiastic performance.

Photos: (top) Lauri Rotko, (right) The Tall Ships Races 2013 Szczecin

Opposite page: Sail Training International

Next page: The Tall Ships Races 2013 Szczecin

PRIZE-GIVING

The crew parade is carefully choreographed so that it ends with the crews arriving at the location of the prize-giving to take their places so that the next phase of the programme can proceed in a timely fashion.

Once the crews are assembled the prize-giving begins with a speech of welcome from the hosts or, in some cases, from the country's president or member of the royal family. The prize-giving ceremony is the highlight of the whole event, with the winners and runners-up in the various classes called up to the stage to receive their awards. The races are closely contested and the race director will have been under some considerable pressure to get the results out quickly after he has checked and rechecked to ensure that they are correct.

There is one prize that remains a closely guarded secret until the moment the winner is revealed at the end of the prize-giving ceremony. This is the Sail Training International Friendship Trophy, presented to the ship that has done the most to promote international understanding and friendship during the race series. The unique thing about this trophy is that the captains and crews of all of the competing ships select the winner by secret ballot. It is the most sought-after trophy in the whole race series and the winning ship is also presented with a flag to fly showing the year that they won the trophy.

Photos: (top) Olli Sulin, (right) Adam Nurkiewicz

Opposite page: Sail Training International

DEWARUCI
Indonesia

LORD NELSON

UNITED KINGDOM

CREW PARTY

Shortly after the prize-giving the crew party starts. This tops off what has been a very busy day and will be the last chance for many of the crews to meet up before they leave their ships and return home the next day. The main ingredients for any successful party are good food, something to drink and music for dancing. The crew party is no different. Where it is different is that it is an occasion when several thousand young people from perhaps 30 to 40 countries will seal the lasting friendships that they have made during the races.

Photos: (this page and opposite) Lauri Rotko

DEPARTURE

After a very full port programme it is often a relief to get back to sea. For new trainee crews this will be their first taste of the ocean and it can be a very varied experience depending almost entirely on the weather they encounter when they leave the port! However, it is a hugely exciting time as the ships traditionally depart in a 'parade of sail'. This is a great spectacle and an important part of the port programme for those watching from the shore and for the large fleet of spectator vessels which like to accompany the parade.

If the organising committee could arrange the ideal parade of sail they would have sunshine and blue skies with just the right amount of wind from the right direction to allow the big and beautiful square-riggers to set all of their sails and glide away in a majestic and breathtaking procession. Sometimes they are lucky; but sometimes there is no wind and the 'parade of sail' becomes, by necessity, a 'parade of engines' with very few sails set. This, however, does not seem to upset the spectators too much as every ship will do its utmost to entertain those watching in a variety of ways, including spectacular Mexican waves with the crew lined up from the bow to the stern. Other ships, particularly the large military square-riggers, have elaborate and rehearsed routines to man the yards and salute the spectators as the ship departs.

After the parade of sail the fleet heads for the race start line and life gets serious as every ship will want to make a good but safe start and many of them will have new crews who have only been on board for a few days. These crews will have had safety briefings and training alongside in the port, including climbing aloft and an introduction to the multitude of ropes, which will become familiar to them over the following days. However, despite all of the training, nothing will have prepared them for the incredible adrenaline rush that accompanies a race start against their new friends on competing vessels.

The race start is a very formalised occasion with strict rules developed by Sail Training International to ensure that it is fair and, more importantly, as safe as such an event can be without taking away the thrill of racing in close company. The chairman of the race committee has the responsibility to decide whether the conditions are suitable for a safe race start. Occasionally starts have to be delayed for a few hours or even a day, but this is usually because there is not enough wind rather than too much.

Once the go-ahead is agreed it is over to the race director to carry out the formal procedures to start each different class, from the big Class A square-riggers to the smaller fast-racing yachts flying spinnaker sails. It is a tense time on the start vessel and a hugely exciting time on board the competing vessels as they manoeuvre for a favourable position while the race director counts down from the ten-minute gun, to the five-minute gun to the start gun – and then they are off, like ocean racehorses, but on a much longer course.

Photos: Max Mudie

Photos: (left) Sail Training International
(top) Rafal Tarakowski
(above) Emmanuel Le Clercq

RACING AT SEA

So now the fleet is at sea, the excitement of the start is over, but the trainees' pulses will still be beating fast as they begin settling into a new and quite unfamiliar routine. They will be in their watches and will have already got to know a little about each other, but will have little idea about how the intensity of this new experience is going to affect each of them and how close they are going to become as a team over the next few days.

First and foremost, despite their different backgrounds and nationalities, they will already have started bonding with the ship as their new home and their shipmates as their new family. They will also be beginning to realise how reliant upon each other they are and the need to work as a team and, more than that, as a team of friends, without which they will not achieve the mission. The mission is not necessarily to win (though that is what they want) but to do their utmost to sail the ship to her maximum speed by skilfully setting and adjusting the sails and sailing a straight course.

Racing on a sail training ship adds a whole new dimension compared with a conventional sail training voyage outside of the races. When racing there is an overwhelming desire to win; the competitive spirit is there in all the young crews, but they are inexperienced and great care has to be taken to ensure that their safety is paramount, without robbing them of the thrill and intense excitement of the racing experience. In addition to harnessing their energy, there is also a need to manage their expectations. Not everyone can be a winner, but the real prize for a racing crew is in knowing that they have done their best.

For the captain and professional crew there will also be a desire to do well and to get the best out of the ship and the inexperienced trainees. Theirs will be the responsibility to consider the weather, the tides and currents and balance these variables with the known capabilities of their ship, to work the crew hard at setting and changing sails to maximise the ship's potential in changing conditions from flat calm to roaring gales, and to do so safely.

At the start of the race the ships are in very close proximity, but very quickly, over just a matter of hours, they draw apart from each other, with the ocean greyhounds forging ahead and the older, more 'comfortable' vessels making a more stately progress. However, on board each different vessel the imperative is the same, to get the very best out of the sailing qualities of the ship. The speed of different vessels varies, but maximising any vessel's potential speed requires the same close attention to sail setting and adjustment.

Generally the fleet will split up into small packs of similarly rated vessels sailing in relatively close company. There will also be races within the main race between sister ships or ships of a similar length and type, many of which have raced against each other for years. This is an added dimension for the race crews who become quite partisan and, while they might not be in the lead in the race overall, they may be fighting another more personal battle with a close rival.

Each day there are twice-daily radio reports from the Sail Training International communications vessel giving the positions of the whole fleet so

Photo: Karl Zilmer

the crews know who is in the lead in the various classes and how they are doing against their closest competitors. They will discover whether their extra special attention to adjusting the sails in the small hours of the morning has been successful!

As they draw closer to the finish line, tensions rise again; not quite to the adrenaline rush of the start but more to do with whether their final attempts at tweaking the sails to get that extra half knot of speed might enable them to overtake their closest rival.

And then it is all over, they have finished the race, they are completely exhausted and suddenly realise how little sleep they have had over the last few days. However, the excitement of being back in port and the anticipation of a few days of fun before they return home soon takes over and very soon they are ashore, meeting up with their new friends and close competitors and discussing tactics like experienced old salts.

Photos: (top) Janine Scheele, (above) Sail Training International

Opposite page: (top) Spirit of Bermuda Archive, (bottom) Max Mudie

Photos: (top) Ad Vermeulen, (above) Rafal Tarakowski

Opposite page: (top) Greg Pease, (bottom) Rienk Boode

REVENUE FOR THE FLEET

Operating a large sailing ship is a very expensive business and Sail Training International sees it as part of its role to help ship operators earn some additional revenue during port visits. The host ports also recognise the need to ensure that a visit by a tall ship is economically beneficial for both parties. Port and event sponsors also like to play their part in helping the fleet earn revenue as part of their visit.

There are a number of ways of achieving this, one of which is for a limited number of ships that are interested to carry out day-sails from the host port for fee-paying passengers. Day-sails, however, are not always popular with the host ports, but when there is a large fleet the odd bit of sailing activity in the dock area can be an added attraction.

Sail Training International has in the past experimented with schemes whereby members of the public can buy tickets to go on board ships in port for a tour. The revenue is then shared between the participating ships. There has also been debate about the principle that the public should not be charged to get into the port area to see the ships. It has always been a firm belief that it should be a 'free show' and, in general, this view extends to going on board the ships that are open to visitors at specific times of the day.

By far the most successful way of raising significant revenue is by taking part in the corporate hospitality schemes organised by most ports. These vary in size and scope, but in their simplest form it means that ships sell their decks to an agent who co-ordinates requests from local companies and businesses that would like to host a dinner or cocktail party for their staff and guests. The opportunity to have a function on board a tall ship surrounded by the rest of the fleet is much sought after and a successful agent will maximise the opportunities during all of the in-port days, both at lunchtime and in the evenings. Sail Training International's commercial directorate is skilled and experienced in helping the ports, the ships and the sponsors to get the very best out of these corporate hospitality opportunities.

MEDIA INTEREST

Harnessing the power of the media in all of its forms is a vital task in promoting the races in advance of the event. This is not just for the benefit of the race organisers but to assist ships in attracting trainees and to promote the race ports so that the international public are aware of the event and can make plans to come and see the fleet. Some host ports are very imaginative in their approach to this. The port of Sochi, Russia, hosts of the SCF Black Sea Tall Ships Regatta 2014, took the event flag and logo to the North Pole for a 'photo opportunity' (top left, opposite page) that received wide coverage, and not just in Russia.

During the event each port sets up a media centre where accredited journalists have access to information about the event, the fleet, the competitors and the port. The media centre is a busy place and is staffed by the port's media staff as well as Sail Training International's media officers. There may also be a desk for representatives of the national sail training organisation to promote local opportunities for sail training.

The media staff will be incredibly busy dealing with several hundred accredited journalists, organising photo opportunities, interviews and news reports. They also arrange press boats to take photographers and film crews to cover the parade of sail and the race start.

The value of media interest generated is measured in terms of printed articles in local, national and international publications, the amount of airtime on television broadcasts and, increasingly, the amount of digital coverage online. These statistics are important when both the event organisers and the ports are seeking commercial sponsorship for the event.

Photos: (top left) Valery Vasilevskiy, (top right and bottom) Sail Training International

TRACKING THE FLEET

If you multiply the several thousand young trainees who take part in a tall ships race by a factor of three to five, for their relatives and friends who want to follow their progress on a daily basis (often several times a day), you have a very large group of people who will be relying upon Sail Training International, as the race organiser, to provide regular reports of the ships' positions.

For many years Sail Training International has embarked communications officers on board an accompanying safety and communications vessel to receive position reports from the fleet twice each day. The position reports are converted to corrected provisional placings, by class and overall, and relayed back to the fleet so that the trainees know whether their efforts at trimming the sails and steering a straight course are paying dividends. These provisional results are posted on the Sail Training International website twice each day so that family and friends are also updated.

New technologies have made it a lot easier to track the fleet and a visit to the Sail Training International website during a race will provide access to a host of different information, not just about the provisional results, but also the location of competing vessels relative to each other in graphic format.

The ships also keep an eye on each other by monitoring the Automatic Identification System (AIS) plots of those vessels that have it fitted, and a great majority of the fleet does, now that it is available at an affordable price for the smaller vessels. Because AIS shows the course and speeds some vessels switch the transmitter off as they think that this information might be advantageous to a competitor!

An increasing number of vessels have their own websites, which include reports from tracking software so that interested relatives and friends can see the position, course and speed of the ship. Some organisations also have 'message boards' on their websites so that messages can be exchanged between those ashore and those afloat.

The Sail Training International system uses a commercial tracking unit fitted to each ship, which automatically transmits her position at regular intervals. All of the positions are plotted so that every vessel's progress can be seen against all of the other competitors on one single chart of the race course, with the sophistication to zoom in and out and to get further detailed information about the vessels, almost in real time.

Photos: (top) Tall Ships America, (bottom) Yellowbrick

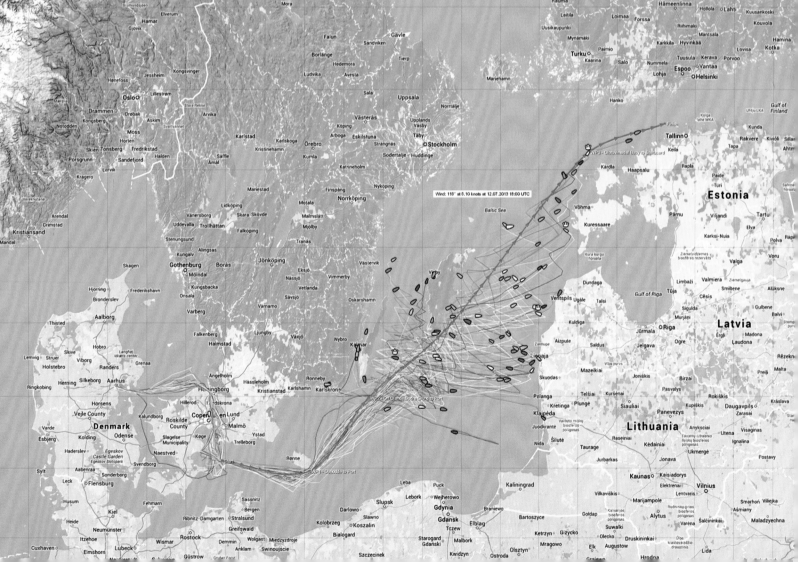

FUNDING FOR TRAINEES

Racing on tall ships has always been popular and will continue to be so, but it is increasingly expensive to manage and maintain the sail training vessels that provide the platform for the adventure. Inevitably the costs have to be passed on, mainly in the form of increased charges for trainee berths. Sail Training International continues to work towards making the sail training experience accessible to everyone, particularly to the more disadvantaged and disabled young people. To this end, a number of bursary schemes have been developed to defray the costs of a voyage for this target group. These schemes have been very successful and are paving the way for further schemes funded by sponsors, host ports and other outside interests that can see the value to young people that a voyage on a sail training vessel can bring. One example is the Sultanate of Oman Bursary Scheme (photo below) that helps to fund the participation of 100 deserving young people in Sail Training International's races every year.

Photo: Sail Training International

INDEX